YOUR HOME
a living canvas

YOUR HOME
a living canvas

CURTIS L. HEUSER

NORTH LIGHT BOOKS
CINCINNATI, OHIO
www.artistsnetwork.com

fw
F+W PUBLICATIONS, INC.

Your Home, A Living Canvas: Create Stunning Faux Finishes and Murals with Paint. Copyright © 2008 by Curtis L. Heuser. Manufactured in China. All rights reserved. The patterns and drawings in this book are for the personal use of the reader. By permission of the author and publisher, they may be either hand-traced or photocopied to make single copies, but under no circumstances may they be resold or republished. It is permissible for the purchaser to paint the designs contained herein and sell them at fairs, bazaars, and craft shows. No other part of this book may be reproduced in any form or by any electronic or mechanical means including information storage and retrieval systems without permission in writing from the publisher, except by a reviewer who may quote brief passages in a review. The content of this book has been thoroughly reviewed for accuracy. However, the author and publisher disclaim any liability for any damages, losses or injuries that may result from the use or misuse of any product or information presented herein. It is the purchaser's responsibility to read and follow all instructions and warnings on all product labels.

Published by North Light Books, an imprint of F+W Publications, Inc., 4700 East Galbraith Road, Cincinnati, Ohio, 45236. (800) 289-0963. First Edition.

Other fine North Light Books are available from your local bookstore, art supply store or direct from the publisher at www.fwbookstore.com.

12   11   10   09   08   5   4   3   2   1

Distributed in Canada by Fraser Direct
100 Armstrong Avenue
Georgetown, ON, Canada L7G 5S4
Tel: (905) 877-4411

Distributed in the U.K. and Europe by David & Charles
Brunel House, Newton Abbot, Devon, TQ12 4PU, England
Tel: (+44) 1626 323200, Fax: (+44) 1626 323319
E-mail: postmaster@davidandcharles.co.uk

Distributed in Australia by Capricorn Link
P.O. Box 704, S. Windsor NSW, 2756 Australia
Tel: (02) 4577-3555

Library of Congress Cataloging-in-Publication Data

Heuser, Curtis L.
    Your home, a living canvas / Curtis L. Heuser. – 1st ed.
        p. cm.
    Subtitle on cover: Create stunning faux finishes and murals with paint
    Includes index.
    ISBN-13: 978-1-58180-783-7 (hc. : alk. paper)
    ISBN-10: 1-58180-783-X (hc. : alk. paper)
    1. Painting. 2. Decoration and ornament. 3. Finishes and finishing. 4. Mural painting and decoration. I.
Title. II. Title: Create stunning faux finishes and murals with paint.
    TT385.H485 2007
    745.7'23–dc22
                                        2007002798

Edited by Vanessa Lyman
Designed by Clare Finney
Photographed by Tim Grondin, Christine Polomsky and Curtis L. Heuser
Production coordinated by Greg Nock

METRIC CONVERSION CHART

To convert	to	multiply by
Inches	Centimeters	2.54
Centimeters	Inches	0.4
Feet	Centimeters	30.5
Centimeters	Feet	0.03
Yards	Meters	0.9
Meters	Yards	1.1

ABOUT THE AUTHOR

Curtis Heuser is one of the Midwest's premier decorative artists, celebrating 20 years in business with the release of this much-anticipated book. He is an expert on custom paint finishes, specializing in fine mural and trompe l'oeil techniques. His finely detailed work has been featured nationally on HGTV's *Around the House* and *Before & After* programs. Curtis transformed interiors from across the country before finally turning his talents to the biggest challenge of all: refurbishing his own historic home, located in Newport, Kentucky. His efforts earned him the City of Newport's "Excellence in Historic Preservation Award" in 2005. Curtis's home has been spotlighted on several public home tours, including the prestigious 2006 Tall Stacks Historic Home Tour, the annual East Row Victorian Christmas Tour, and the Home Builder's Association of Northern Kentucky Tour of Remodeled Homes. Curtis also offers private group tours of his home, as well as occasional public workshops and demonstrations of his craft. His website is www.livingmurals.com.

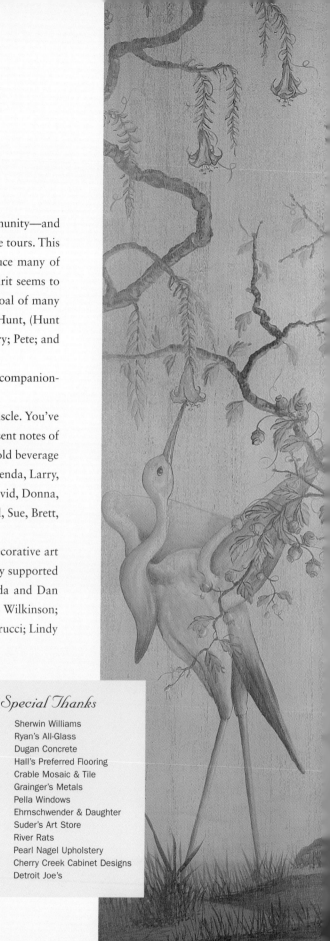

I dedicate this book to my mother, Clara Heuser, whose kindred spirit will live forever in my heart. I love you, Mom!

ACKNOWLEDGEMENTS

The most rewarding aspect of this project has been sharing this adventure with family, friends and community—and now with you! My "living canvas" (as people call my home) has been included in several neighborhood home tours. This has afforded me wonderful opportunities to meet countless neighbors and new friends and also to introduce many of them to the creative splendor of decorative painting. People are inspired by this home—and that artistic spirit seems to be contagious! The countless hours and intense effort put into revitalizing this property has been a shared goal of many local craftspeople and specialty contractors. My wholehearted gratitude goes to my general contractor, Joe Hunt, (Hunt Custom Remodeling, LLC), and his fine network of subcontractors, especially Jon; Ken, Sr.; Ken, Jr.; Jim; Jerry; Pete; and Cory. Spectacular job, guys!

A loving thank you to friend and fellow decorative artist, Robin Harrison, whose expert assistance and companionship during this project kept me sane. I couldn't have done it without you, darling!

I fondly appreciate and thank my dear friends and family, who generously volunteered both time and muscle. You've done a little of everything: organized the massive yard sale; demolished, cleaned and painted; led home tours; sent notes of encouragement; arrived at a moment's notice to take a picture for me; even dropped by unexpectedly with a cold beverage and a hot meal! Thanks for all your heartfelt encouragement and support, especially: Mom (Clara), Linda, Brenda, Larry, Harold, Eric, Lori, Tim, Robin, Jeff, Steve, Meg and Mike, Marvin, Dianne, David L. and Gary, Robb and David, Donna, Jim and Emery, Denny, Robert, Israel, Adam, Steve B., John and Rita, Bill and Diane, Sandy, Rachel, Ed, Paul, Sue, Brett, Kim, Joby, Sharon, Carol, Ros, Aaron, Barbie and Brad.

I'm grateful to have shared my God-given talents with all the many patrons, who have supported my decorative art business since its start in 1987. I especially wish to thank the following patrons who believed in and generously supported this unique undertaking: Kerry and Russ Mock; Anne and Kurt Lundblad; Barbara and Dick Bruder; Linda and Dan Whittenburg; Linda and Steve Schuler; Jeanne Corwin and Mark Deutsch; Lisa and Kevin Fitzgerald; Kathy Wilkinson; Donna and Dean Trindle; Michelle and Greg Young; Roseanne and Don Beckmeyer; Marianne and Matt Castrucci; Lindy and Steve Wyatt; Rebecca Walker Drouhard; Larry Johnson and Tom Ridgeway.

Finally, I wish to sincerely thank everyone at F+W Publications who helped bring this book together. I am especially grateful to Clare Finney, my wonderfully creative art director and neighbor; she introduced my talent to F+W, turning me into an aspiring new author! Kudos to photographer Tim Grondin and his assistants, Bethany Vail and Tara Trullinger, for producing magnificent beauty shots of my home. Warm thanks to my editor, Vanessa Lyman, who recaptured the initial spirit and enthusiasm behind *Your Home, A Living Canvas*, then fine-tuned it and released it here for your enjoyment! To Jamie Markle: Thank you for being so understanding of all the unforeseen obstacles and misfortunes that caused me to miss a few deadlines. This has been a wonderful and truly life-changing experience; I'm honored to have been given such an extraordinary opportunity.

Special Thanks

Sherwin Williams
Ryan's All-Glass
Dugan Concrete
Hall's Preferred Flooring
Crable Mosaic & Tile
Grainger's Metals
Pella Windows
Ehrnschwender & Daughter
Suder's Art Store
River Rats
Pearl Nagel Upholstery
Cherry Creek Cabinet Designs
Detroit Joe's

CONTENTS

FOYER. 16

As a visitor's first and last impression of your home, the foyer should be a warm and inviting area. Embossed wainscoting with faux bronzed patina, a torn-tissue wall finish and fantasy marble panels help showcase the foyer's star—the grand, original oak staircase. The atmosphere of the foyer is alluring and captures the warm, artistic spirit of the house. Welcome to my home!

PARLOR 30

This room has a distinguished, opulent charm that sets a dignified tone for the house. The focal point is a massive fireplace with a trompe l'oeil carved limestone mantel and a custom-made, stained-glass mosaic surround. For a formal feel, I used a lavish, faux linen-damask finish. Antiqued crown molding creates a nice transition to the rest of the house.

DINING ROOM. 42

The dining room's central location inspired me to transform it into a gathering place for family and friends. From a faux-fresco frieze and rustic, faux-pickled finish wall panels to a vintage pressed-tin panel with a terra cotta faux finish and a dimensional starburst ceiling medallion, the dining room offers a feast for the guests' eyes.

KITCHEN 56

To make the kitchen the heart of the house, I wanted to create an environment rich in color and texture, yet lighthearted in mood and overall atmosphere. A custom wall mural, trompe l'oeil tiled backsplash and faux-fresco range hood warm the comfortable and functional space. Above the scene, three massive faux-wood-grained beams further define the kitchen with a Tuscan-inspired theme.

STUDY & OFFICE 74

These two rooms really push the "wow" factor with a number of visual elements. You will find faux-leather walls, a faux limestone wall, a faux wood-grained mantel, crackle-finish bookcases, a monochromatic figurative mural on the ceiling and a faux-bronzed ceiling medallion. The subtle relationships between the finishes create a dramatic, peaceful atmosphere for work or relaxation.

GUESTROOM 94

It is a lucky guest that rests in this bedroom, enveloped by its tranquil beauty and irresistible charm. The full-room, chinoiserie-inspired mural sets the tone and transports guests to a Chinese garden, inspiring their imaginations. Custom window- and bed-dressings, wall-to-wall carpeting, fireplace and antique furnishings, all serve to elegantly pamper overnight guests.

MASTER SUITE. 116

The third floor boasts a luxurious master suite, complete with a graceful cathedral ceiling. Features include faux-wood, railroad-tie beams; a spacious, custom-built, walk-in closet; a deluxe master bath; and an intimate, yet functional art studio area. Some walls feature trompe l'oeil drapes over a rag-textured finish while others have a faux river-stone finish. Distressed built-in cabinets with a warm, mellow patina help make the most of the awkwardly shaped room.

INTRODUCTION

L IFE HAS AN ODD WAY OF PLAYING OUT SOMETIMES. Take how my home and this book got started, for instance. In late May 2002, I noticed a "For Sale" sign on the house on the corner of Eighth Street and Park Avenue in the charming East Row Historic District of Newport, Kentucky. I came to the neighborhood in order to add period charm to a client's lovely Victorian home and immediately fell in love with the neighborhood's varied architectural styles: Victorian, Italianate, Gothic Revival, Queen Anne with traditional and Romanesque detailing. . .

Almost every evening, I walked my dogs, Tippy and Frankie, through the neighborhood, stopping to admire the houses. One in particular, a corner residence, had wonderful architectural potential. I was attracted by the sensuous curve of the brick wall flanking one side of the house, and the gracious front entrance and side porches. Beyond those elements, the old corner house seemed sad, standing so proud and yet in obvious need of loving care. The towering third floor gables had been covered with aluminum siding, hiding the unique side windows, as well as the original scalloped, wooden shakes deteriorating beneath. The roof, though fairly new, was unattractive and historically inappropriate. Finally, the property was engulfed by overgrown maple trees that seemed to smother the house.

Little did I know that I would soon buy this magnificent house and inherit all of its magnificent ailments. My cousin Marsha, a real estate agent, showed me the property. When we stepped inside, we were immediately assailed by the stench of molding carpet. There wasn't much to endear me to the interior: crumbling plaster walls; dark 1960s paneling; dropped ceilings fitted with fluorescent lights; and heavy nicotine-stained drapes that obliterated any natural light. But I could still see opportunities; the bones of the house were there and seemed promising.

The home was sold with its contents, and it contained a lot: it was literally filled to the rafters with old furniture, clothing still in the closets, old mattresses, boxes of knickknacks, bicycles, lawn mower parts, even canned food in the pantry. It was so jammed, I completely overlooked the fireplace in the guest bedroom. The bank appraiser, I later discovered, missed the entire third floor!

I saw all of this, right down to the small lake that had formed in the dingy, boarded-up basement; but there was a spirit to the house that welcomed me in. I wanted to restore its glory and make it my home, a place where everyone would feel that welcoming spirit.

My offer of $95,000 was counter-offered at $97,800; and the rest is history.

One of the first things I did was have a yard sale to clear out all the junk. As serendipity would have it, Clare Finney (art director for North Light Books) came to the yard sale and noticed the sign on my truck: Curtis Heuser, Decorative Artist. Clare came over to talk to me; I showed her my portfolio; and she invited me to meet with the editorial staff the following week.

And so the story of the house's rebirth into my home came to be documented in this book, *Your Home, A Living Canvas*. I hope it offers hands-on insight into the process of reinventing an old home. Most importantly, I hope it inspires and encourages you, whether you're interested in learning simple faux-finish techniques, or are dedicated to preserving the architecture and charm of a historic community. I share with you the long, artistic journey to transform a house into the place I fondly call "home."

The Transformed Home. The corner house, once sadly in need of loving care, is now a stately home. As a historic house, its charm is preserved; as my home, it is beautiful, comfortable and welcoming.

MATERIALS

PAINTS

Most paints used in this book are manufactured by Sherwin Williams. I've provided a color swatch as well as the paint's name to help you in making as exact a match as possible. The type of surface you are working on should determine the type of paint or primer you use.

PRIMERS

Bare plaster/drywall or painted walls: Use a high grade latex primer. I prefer Sherwin Williams PrepRite 200 Interior Latex Primer.

Bare or old painted wood: Use a high-grade oil/alkyd-based primer. I prefer Sherwin Williams PrepRite ProBlock.

Areas prone to moisture (such as a laundry room or bathroom): I recommend using a product like KILZ Premium, a fabulous interior/exterior, water-based sealer, primer and stain blocker formulated specifically for moisture-prone environments.

Switch plates and outlet covers: Spray primer is ideal to use on switch plates, air vents and outlet coverings. Because I find them unsightly, I always paint over these. First, I remove the cover, then lightly sand or scuff it up. I wipe off the residue and lightly spray on two coats of primer. I prefer Sherwin Williams PrepRite SF-1 Quick Drying Alkyd Primer/Sealer but B-I-N and KILZ also work.

PAINTS

Walls to be basecoated: I always use a latex satin finish product, like Sherwin Williams SuperPaint Interior Latex Satin Paint. The subtle sheen of the paint when dry is more attractive than the traditional "flat" finish and easier to clean and maintain. Satin is also an ideal finish on which to apply faux and mural work. The slightly slick surface extends the workable or "open" time for glazes, color washes, etc., since it's not as absorbent as flat-sheen paints. For faux finishing, a satin, eggshell, semigloss or gloss surface will all cover easily. Experiment with each of these sheens to learn the differences.

Ceilings: For ceilings, a flat-sheen latex paint is preferable. The flat finish hides imperfections and gives the surface more depth. (A reflective surface, on the other hand, bounces light and creates the illusion of less height in a room.) I prefer Sherwin Williams ProMar 200 Interior Latex Flat Paint.

Trim, doors and cabinetry: For these surfaces, especially if they're bare wood, I prefer to apply an oil/alkyd-based paint product. I like Sherwin Williams' semigloss ProClassic Enamel paint.

Staircases: For a frequently used surface like a stairwell, acrylic enameled based paints work best. The acrylic hardness creates a very durable scuff and chip resistant finish. Sherwin Williams All Surface Enamel black latex satin paint worked wonderfully on the staircase kickboards and as an accent color throughout the piece.

Spray paints: For the stenciling on the foyer walls, I used the quickest method to transfer the stencil—spraying. Do It Best spray paint in Metallic Gold produces an intense, metallic glow.

Behlen Jet Spray toner: This product is normally used on wood surfaces to help blend old and new wood, but I use it to add the appearance of patina and age to painted finishes.

TINTING GLAZES

To tint oil glaze, I prefer an oil-based, semigloss paint, like Sherwin Williams ProClassic Alkyd Interior Enamel. I add a small amount of the enamel to the oil glazing liquid until the desired tone is achieved. I prefer this method over using universal tinters because the oil paint blends more easily when mixing; and the resulting color, though a translucent glaze, is truer and more vibrant. This formula also removes the guesswork if you need to restore or touch up a glazed area. I also prefer the semigloss finish, when mixed with the oil glaze, as it dries to a soft luster.

STAINS

Wood stains are ideal for antiquing painted surfaces and are available in a variety of tints. To apply, brush on, then wipe using a cloth dampened with mineral spirits, leaving color in the crevices of the painted detail. The drawback to using wood stain on a painted surface is that the stain cannot penetrate the surface like it does with wood, so it can take longer to fully dry. I used Minwax Wood Finish in Provincial no. 211, to add an attractive, aged effect to the painted chair rail in the foyer.

I also used Sherwin Williams Wood Classics Interior Oil Stain and Minwax Pre Stain Wood Conditioner for the dining room paneled walls.

SEALERS

Most painted finishes look better with a finishing coat of clear polyurethane. I prefer to use one with a soft, low-luster sheen, like Minwax's water-based Polycrylic Protective Finish. This product is extremely durable (it's made primarily to protect floors) and is fast-drying, allowing for multiple coats in one setting. Most importantly, it's non-yellowing, so it has a minimal effect on the final color.

PAINT MEDIUMS

Floetrol: Floetrol Waterborne Paint Conditioner is a latex paint additive that promotes smooth paint application. It also enhances the fluidity of water-based paint, giving the painter more time to manipulate the surface with faux applications (e.g., ragging and mottling). I add Floetrol to latex color wash mixtures to help maintain a wet working edge.

Paints: 1. Latex satin house paint in plastic containers. **2.** Lincrusta®. **3.** Square-tipped artist's brushes (brights). **4.** Pouncing brush. **5.** Do It Best spray paint. **6.** Square stippling brush. **7.** Chip brushes. **8.** Sherwin Williams Illusions oil glaze, MinWax Polycrylic sealer and Sherwin Williams interior satin paint. **9.** Strié brush. **10.** Artist's rounded tip detail brushes. **11.** Spray bottle. **12.** Badger hair softening brush. **13.** Paint pan. **14.** Angled cutting-in brush. **15.** Standard roller with sponge cover. **16.** Sherwin Williams color chart. **17.** MinWax wood stain.

Oil-Based Glazing Liquid: Color glazes for faux finishing can be either latex or oil-based. I prefer to use oil-based glazes because of its longer "open" time for faux finishing or manipulating a surface. I use Sherwin Williams Illusions Faux Finish Glazing Liquid. Most of my glazes consist of a formula of 75% oil-based glazing liquid to 25% mineral spirits, with custom-colored oil paint added slowly until the desired translucency is achieved. Always test the strength of your mixture atop the base color to ensure the correct tone.

Mineral Spirits: Oil paint thinner, also called mineral spirits, is ideal for making stainlike, oil-tinted color washes. Simply mix mineral spirits with any oil-based paint until you achieve the desired translucency. You can add linseed oil to the mixture and oil varnish or polyurethane to create an even more authentic, custom-colored stain. I often add mineral spirits to liquid glaze and oil tint, for various faux-finishing techniques such as strié and rag rolling. By experimenting with the amounts you add to a glaze, you can quickly learn how to mix the proper formulas for creating countless effects. Mineral spirits is also used to clean oil-based residue from brushes, tools and even hands!

Water: Latex or water-based paints can be easily transformed into luminous, watercolor-like washes by simply adding water. I often use a water spritzer bottle to keep the wall ahead of me damp as I apply latex paint washes. Latex color washes add tremendous depth and atmosphere to any space. By adding more water to the paint, you increase its fluidity and "open" time. This is important when feathering out tones or texturing the wash with dampened rags or sponges.

STRIPPERS/CLEANERS

Denatured Alcohol: To restore the staircase, I removed the shellacked, old finish by rubbing it vigorously with S-L-X Denatured Alcohol. The unsightly, discolored finish dissolved easily and I was left with a clean surface, with little residue, ready for refinishing.

FAUX EFFECTS PRODUCTS

SetCoat/Clear: Seals the walls, giving the other faux products longer "open" time.

AquaSize/Clear: An undercoat application that reacts with the crackle coat, creating a finish.

AquaCrackle/Clear: A top coat medium that is tinted to the desired crackle color.

Faux Effects products

FauxCreme: A water-based glazing liquid that can be tinted with crème color tints (below).

FauxCreme Color: Colorants that allow you to custom tint your glaze.

Magic Metallic and Modern Masters products

Activator II: A chemical activator that reacts with the top layer of glaze and embeds waterlike droplet patterns into the finish.

Porcelain Crackle: Crackle medium that produces finer crackling results than ordinary crackle glaze.

MAGIC METALLIC AND MODERN MASTERS PRODUCTS

Copper Metallic (MM-102) and Dark Bronze Metallic (MM-103): Specialty paint formulated for simulating metal surfaces. These paints are designed to react with Rapid Rust (MM-305), a chemical activating medium, to form actual rust deposits.

Metallic Paint: I use Modern Masters Metallic Paint in Antique Bronze (ME-204) to create certain aged patinas.

BRUSHES

I like to work with a selection of inexpensive, natural-bristle "chip" brushes ranging in size from 1- to 3-inches (25mm to 75mm). These can be thrown away, which saves time during cleanup. Chip brushes are great for feathering out colors, drybrushing and applying glazes and stains. The drawback to using them is that they shed easily, leaving loose hairs in the paint. You can control this problem by tumbling the brush vigorously between your hands to remove loose hairs.

ADDITIONAL BRUSHES:

- A few high-grade angled sash brushes (nylon-polyester blend) for cutting in paints and glazes.
- A 7 ½-inch (19cm) strié or weaving brush. This creates fine streaks in a glaze when dragged through the wet surface. You can substitute a nylon wallpaper nylon brush for a more rigid, linear effect.
- A selection of small round, soft-haired artist's brushes. Nos. 0, 1, and 8 hold paint well and allow for great detail.
- A selection of ¼-inch (6mm) to 1-inch (25mm) flat-bristle brushes. I use these to drybrush details on ornamentation and raised decorations.
- A selection of square-tipped "brights"—fine artist's brushes made of soft oxen hair. I used these brushes for all mural work in this book. They hold paint well and can stand up to a solid drywall surface.
- Mach One Striper, or pin-striping brush, made of soft squirrel hair. This brush is used for laying-in marble veining. It holds a lot of paint, and creates quirky thin or thick lines, depending on the amount of pressure applied.

- Badger-hair softening brush. This is a fairly expensive brush that has long, soft bristles and is used for feathering out brushstrokes and blending color, especially when marbling.
- Old, stiff painter's brush for stippling.
- 4-inch (100mm)-diameter round pouncing brush for blending and mottling color glazes.
- Long-haired artist's detail brush.

ADDITIONAL PAINT APPLICATION TOOLS

Assortment of rollers and covers:

- 9-inch (23cm) standard roller.
- ½-inch (12mm) nap covers for lint-free coating application.
- Mohair covers for applying smooth oil-glazing coatings.
- Sponge roller covers for applying and evening out oil glazes.
- 6-inch (15cm) whiz roller, with both fabric and foam covers, for paint and glaze coats.
- Selection of foam brushes, including 1-inch (25mm), 2-inch (51mm), 3-inch (75mm) and 4-inch (100mm) for applying paint and lifting activator.
- Paint sticks for mixing.
- Clear container for holding water.
- Metal paint tray and disposable clear liners for easy cleanup.

- Lightweight foam dinner plates to use as palettes.
- Plastic and fabric drop clothes for protecting furniture and floors.
- Covered mixing containers for mixing and storing glazes and color washes.
- Paint grid for putting into paint can to drain off excess paint or glaze from the roller.
- Broadcloth, a crisp cotton/polyester fabric for creating perfect rag-rolling texture.
- Cheesecloth for adding interesting texture to painted finishes.
- Cotton rags for mottling paints and glazes.
- Paper towels for easy wiping and clean up.

TEXTURING MATERIALS

Sheetrock Lightweight All Purpose Joint Compound: I use joint compound throughout this book as my preferred material for texturing surfaces. It is used for many projects, from simulating thick, knotty-grained wood beams to forming a custom, three-dimensional ceiling medallion. An inexpensive five-gallon (four-liter) container will last a long time for small projects.

The material is very forgiving and can be easily wiped off with a damp rag. When it dries, it's easy to paint and distress joint compound with ordi-

Brushes: 1. Chinese calligraphy brush with bamboo handle. **2.** Selection of soft-bristled, artists "round" brushes. **3.** Selection of square-tipped, artists "bright" brushes.

nary paints and sandpaper. It can be tinted, color washed or glazed without being primed.

Venetian Plaster: Venetian plaster is a specially formulated, premixed texture that is troweled on, layered and burnished to achieve a wonderful polished, marble-like finish. I prefer to use Behr Venetian Plaster because it's affordable and readily available at home improvement stores.

APPLICATORS AND TOOLS

- 12-inch (30cm) plastic mud pan—for mixing joint compound.
- 12-inch (30cm) blue steel taping knife—to hold joint compound as it's applied.
- Flexible steel joint/putty knife selection—a 1 ½-inch (37mm), 3-inch (7.5cm) angled blade, 4-inch (10cm) and 6-inch (15cm) assortment is adequate.

- Set of Venetian plaster blue thin steel spatulas—specially designed for applying Venetian plaster.
- Selection of artist's palette knives—for applying texture to small detailed areas.
- Two 'Fer Opener—makes opening 5-gallon (4-liter) buckets of joint compound or paint easy.
- Paint/joint compound mixer—can be attached to a drill to quickly mix tints into the product.

Texturing Materials: 1. Steel wool. **2.** Behr Venetian plaster. **3.** Flexible steel putty knives. **4.** Artist's palette knives. **5.** Venetian plaster blue steel spatulas. **6.** Blue steel taping knife. **7.** Two 'Fer Opener. **8.** Caulking gun. **9.** Electric drill with mixing extension. **10.** Natural sponges. **11.** Steel ticking roller. **12.** Blue steel graining combs. **13.** Sandpapers. **14.** Joint compound. **15.** Plastic mud pan.

GENERAL MATERIALS

There's an endless array of products for decorative painting on the market. Obviously, the best way to learn about them is through trial and error. After 20 years in this industry, however, I've discovered a few key items that are generally useful to keep on hand: latex paintable caulking and caulking gun, tape measure, tracing paper pad and roll, tissue sheets, graphite paper for transferring designs, sandpaper, colored chalk, utility and craft knives, spray adhesive for attaching stencil to wall, steel ticking roller, blue steel-toothed wood-graining combs, wood filler and spackling (for patching imperfections), colored and graphite pencils.

GILDING MATERIALS

For gilding, I use these materials: Ronan Aqua Leaf, Imitation Dutch Metal, Wunda Size (water-based), a soft brush for applying leaf, cotton balls for burnishing the leaf to the surface.

TAPES

- Scotch brand blue painter's tape in ¾-inch (1.9cm), 2-inch (5cm) and 1 ½-inch (3.75cm) widths. This tape typically won't disturb previously painted surfaces. It has low tack but leaves clean edges.
- Easy Mask, white "Kleen Edge" low tack tape. Leaves extremely clean edges and is great for use around delicate ceilings.
- ¼-inch (6mm) automotive pin striping detail tape.

General Materials: 1. Mineral spirits paint thinner. **2.** Lidded containers. **3.** Floetrol latex paint extender. **4.** Cheesecloth. **5.** Colored chalk. **6.** Carbon paper. **7.** Tracing paper. **8.** Level. **9.** Hair dryer. **10.** Drywall and wood spackling. **11.** Scissors. **12.** Disposable gloves. **13.** Spray adhesives. **14.** Sizing. **15.** Spray wood toner. **16.** Dutch metal sheets. **17.** Eyewear. **18.** Various tapes. **19.** Kneepads. **20.** Spray primer. **21.** Measuring tape and ruler. **22.** Colored pencils. **23.** Craft and utility knives. **24.** Permanent marker.

FOYER

THE FOYER overflows with warm, inviting color and period charm. There are all kinds of decor details in the foyer to draw a visitor in. Textured walls the color of sun-drenched gold contrast dramatically with the dark wood of the furniture and accessories. The delicate colors of a hand-painted chair rail frame a vividly painted Lincrusta® wainscoting. The undisputed jewel of the room, however, is the finely appointed original oak staircase. Its twisting hand-turned spiral spindles and fluted newel posts define the space. The staircase rises majestically against the towering 21-foot (6.4m) wall of bronze-tinted mirror. The somber tone of the reflection is lightened with the long, colorful, faux-marbled panels. The landing at the top of the steps glows with color streaming from the stunning stained glass window. The atmosphere of the foyer is alluring and captures the warm, artistic spirit of the house. Welcome to my home!

Foyer Before. The original passageways that led to the dining room and basement stairs had been closed off.

Foyer During Demolition. In order to return the space to its original floor plan, nearly every interior wall and ceiling in the house had to be torn out and reconfigured. Sadly, the old lath slats fell with the severely damaged original plaster walls, as seen here.

Foyer During Construction. With the floor tiles installed and the walls plastered, the foyer already looks vastly improved. The hallway extends to the back of the house now, opening up the room to give the foyer the dramatic space it needs.

Recessed Niche. (Above) A cast polyurethane, arched niche was installed in the middle of the long corridor to add a "nostalgic" flair to the setting. The niche separates the entrances to the powder room and cloak closet (both tucked below the rising stairs).

Foyer Completed. (At right) After the remodeling, the foyer glows with warmth and period charm. The deeply saturated amber walls combine with the gently distressed, rich verdigris wainscoting to set the stage. Contrasting natural wood tones in the antique furniture and refurbished staircase further enrich the setting.

Definitely Not a Dime a Dozen. While demolishing the foyer, we found this dime from 1890 carefully positioned in a circular cut-out under the base molding. Presumably, it was placed there as a reminder of the year the house was constructed.

Details Define the Setting

Arched symmetry. The entrance to the dining room (back left) echoes the gracefully arched, original stained glass transom above the front door. I chose to arch this opening as a diversion from all the other, more typical squared-off entrances in the foyer. The uniqueness adds architectural interest, and its symmetry with the original transom connects the new with the past.

Antique accents. Among the other antique furnishings in the foyer, the heavily carved console and grandfather clock are late eighteenth century. The arched, beveled glass doors on the clock and the carved heraldic motifs on the console are Gothic in nature.

Acanthus pattern. The acanthus leaf—a favorite Italian decorating motif—appears in the pattern of the stair runner and in the newel finials. Stylized versions of the motif, as you will see, are repeated throughout the house.

THE GRAND STAIRWELL AND STAINED GLASS

Finding an original, almost intact staircase in a home built over 100 years ago is a rare discovery. The first time I stepped into the foyer, this magnificent ascension had my heart pounding!

Restoring the staircase proved to be a long and exhausting task—it took well over 100 man hours to complete. Missing components, like the newel post finials, had to be found and finished to blend with the old. I found a wealth of suitable reproduction replacements by simply browsing the Internet. Surprisingly, the ancient, shellac-based finish on the wooden spindles and railings scrubbed off fairly easily with a little denatured alcohol. Some of the grime was carefully left behind—I didn't want to disturb the stairwell's well-earned wrinkles. I did "freshen up" the overall look of the stairwell by painting the sides and kick boards of the steps with an ebony paint finish. I then lightly drybrushed a rust-colored paint here and there over the ebony finish. This softened the relationship with the natural wood tones of the refinished railings and spindles. The completed staircase now has a formal "Biedermeier" appearance, as reflected in the mirrored walls.

Stairwell Before. Though intact, the stairwell was missing newel post finials and trim detail. It was showing its age, with deeply gouged and splintered handrails and dangling, loose spindles.

Stairwell After. The resin embellishments are simple to apply and add to the distinguished air of the staircase. Their design plays on the acanthus leaf theme threaded throughout the house.

Stairwell After. I added the finial to the newel post, staining it in a manner similar to the resin embellishments. The newel post is hollow and will hold a time capsule which will include mementoes showing the transformation of the house.

Staircase Landing Before. The top of the arched window had been previously covered from the outside with siding. It had also been fitted with a hideous aluminum storm window. The nearby house is plainly visible in the background.

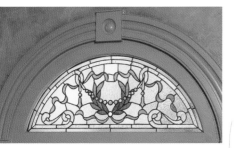

Transom. This is the only original stained glass in the home. Missing pieces were carefully matched, and the entire window was cleaned and releaded. The laurel leaf wreath motif—this one accented with a flowing ribbon and a string of amber pearls—was a common design element of the Victorian era.

Staircase Landing After. The new window design combines the Gothic arch with a lush garden view of old-fashioned purple irises and pink dogwood blossoms. Three songbirds play about the scene. The design reflects my love and respect for nature.

Inscription. The window's inscription encapsulates how I feel about my home and this book, as well as creative success and personal happiness.

The staircase landing was home to a very dull and rather ugly stained glass window, one far too modern and geometric for this home. Because it wasn't original to the home, I felt comfortable replacing it with a window of my own design. The inscription—Seed inspiration, Nurture with Passion and Life blooms abundantly—is my own; it encompasses how I feel about this house and book, as well as my beliefs toward creative success and personal happiness. Dave Ehrnschwender constructed this stunning window, developing the design, from a quick pencil sketch of mine. He was able to recycle some of the old colored glass from the previous window, inserting it into the arched border of the new design. The window reflects my affection for botanical and wildlife art and floods the landing with color (as well as blocking out the unsightly view of the house next door!).

Dave also restored the arched, stained glass transom, original to the home, above the front entrance. The colored glass had become clouded and loose, and some of the pieces—including the leading—were no where to be found. The newly restored window glows above the front door as a true testament of time: it has continually greeted guests to the home for over a century!

I tend to illuminate rooms with various types of lighting: recessed lights, chandeliers, wall sconces, picture lights, and occasional lamps. Having several types of lighting in a room allows you to control the room's tone: brightly illuminated or dramatically aglow, as a special occasion may warrant. (Dimmer switches should be installed whenever possible.) For all the fixed or permanent fixtures in the home, I chose Gothic styled pieces, which were commonly found in the Italianate architecture of the Victorian period. As luck would have it, while antiquing with friends in Lawrenceburg, Indiana, I stumbled across a wonderful collection of old wall sconces and pendant chandeliers salvaged from a demolished church. As an early house-warming gift, my friends rewired and replated all the fixtures, an expenditure well worth the investment. The refurbished, gleaming brass and copper fixtures—now flanking the dining room entrance and the guest bedroom's door in the hallway above—feel right at home. The one oversized sconce perfectly illuminates the landing. I decided to use the pair of pendant chandeliers to light the kitchen galley (see page 61); they incorporated the Gothic theme into the more rustic kitchen. Placed on top of the Gothic-styled antique console (another antique market bargain) (see opposite page), a pair of traditional accent lamps wear a sleek, black and gold, "crackle" paint finish. The pair cast a gentle illumination onto the rare, antique sepia toned photograph hanging above.

The flooring is another subtle but vital element in the room's character. The striking, neutral-toned stone travertine floor is installed on a diagonal. Setting the tiles on a diagonal gives the room the illusion of more width and depth. Using the larger 18" × 18" (45cm × 45cm) travertine tiles keeps the design from looking too busy. The smaller border around the room helps define the space

The diagonal pattern is accented with a terra cotta-toned floret detail in tumbled marble. The florets were hand-cut from a pre-assembled mosaic border that I found at a local home improvement store.

The shimmering granite tiles in the passageways are outlined by the tumbled-marble, mosaic border. This combination adds emphasis to the passageways and gives a sense of opulence to the open floor plan. The terra cotta accent tones—in both the granite and marble—make for a warm transition into the newly installed, Brazilian rosewood floors in the adjacent parlor and dining room.

Main Light Source. The main light source is a lantern-like chandelier with wonderfully wavy and pitted glass. Even though I found it at a local home discount store, when connected with the carved medallion, it feels like it belonged there forever.

Light for the Landing. The one oversized sconce was a perfect fit for the landing by the stained glass window.

Welcome Light. The antique, Gothic-inspired wall sconces—salvaged from a demolished church—cast a warm glow into the foyer. They were replated and rewired and now welcome guests into the house with their warm glow.

The Gothic Arch. Gothic arches dominate this picturesque scene in the entry hall. Notice the arched pillared colonnade perspective in the sepia-toned vintage photograph detailing the interior of the church of Saint Paul in Rome. The arch motif is repeated in the decorative wooden box. The passageway to the dining room furthers the arch motif.

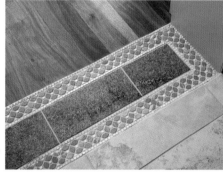

Passageway to Dining Room. Stone, marble, granite and hardwood harmonize as you enter the dining room.

Tumbled-marble Mosaic Strip. Individual florets were hand cut from this tumbled marble border and used as corner accents on the travertine floor.

Field Tile. The field tile in the foyer is composed of 18" × 18" (45cm × 45cm) natural stone travertine.

EMBOSSED WAINSCOTING WITH FAUX BRONZE PATINA

Restoring the architectural details was a challenging aspect of this home's renovation. I believe the right details are essential in making any home, but even more so in the case of a period home. So began my odyssey for period lighting, stained glass windows, flooring, crown moldings and specialty trims. When looking for a surface to place under the new chair railing, I came across this wonderful Lincrusta® paper at a Sherwin Williams store. It reminded me of the original embossed leather wainscoting I had seen at a nearby open house.

Invented during the late Victorian period as an alternative to the more expensive tooled leathers and pressed tin, Lincrusta® is a heavily embossed material you can apply to any wall, much like wall paper. The delicate, embossed floret pattern adds yet another textured dimension to the layered feel of the room.

In order to be preserved, the Lincrusta® must be painted, so I embellished it with a faux bronze patina. The result resembles vintage pressed tin paneling, a prized architectural feature originally found in homes from this period.

MATERIALS LIST

Roller; 2-inch (51mm) chip brush; water spray bottle; Lincrusta® (Sherwin Williams); a glaze or polyurethane protective coat; rag

Sherwin Williams Palette: 1. Coconut Husk 2. Restful 3. Gold Crest

1 **Mount the Lincrusta®.** Apply the Lincrusta® to the wall following the manufacturer's instructions.

2 **Basecoat the Lincrusta®.** Roll on the coconut-colored base coat.

3 **Mist a working area.** After the base coat has thoroughly dried, lightly mist a working area.

4 **Apply a verdigris finish.** Double load a 2-inch (51mm) chip brush with blue green and gold latex colors. Starting just below the chair rail, 'streak' the colors randomly in a downward sweeping motion, varying the intensity of the color. To make the colors blend more easily, occasionally spritz the working area with water. The water will also thin the paint as it's applied to the surface, allowing the brown base coat to "ghost" through.

5 **Distress the finish.** To reinforce the Lincrusta®'s beautiful raised detailing, gently wipe the surface before it completely dries with a damp rag. Don't scrub too hard or you may remove the base coat as well; if this happens, touch up the area with the paint and a small artist's brush. It's always a good idea to test a technique in a smaller, unnoticeable corner first. When this working area is dry, apply a coat of polyurethane to protect, seal and even out the finish.

A LITTLE INSPIRATION

Restoring the interior and exterior features of a historic property is a challenge, but searching for the perfect details can also be exciting. For inspiration, I found it very helpful to frequent local real estate open houses, custom builder's home-a-ramas, designer showhouses and my favorite local library and bookstores. I took good notes along the way and soon found myself compiling individual files for each room. I included my notes, but also all kinds of other inspirational tidbits: images collected from my favorite home decorating magazines, as well as photo references of each room from all angles; fabric samples; appliance information and wish lists; precise room measurements and a floor plan; lighting options; paint chips and color inspiration; samples of interiors I admired; furniture references; accessories and unusual arrangements of collections; window coverings; and samples of architectural details. The files were invaluable resources for visually communicating with everyone from contractors to store personnel.

The Verdigris Patina. A verdigris patina forms on bronze and copper as the result of exposure to sun, rain and air, which oxidizes the metal. It's a highly desirable look associated with antiquity because it can take generations for the mellow blue-green patina to fully mature. Unless you can wait that long, knowing how to get the look with paint—almost in a matter of minutes—is a handy skill to learn. I have applied this finish on everything from simple picture frames, to old, concrete garden relics. Metallic base coats like copper, brass or bronze will create an even more convincing patina, especially on smaller objects. I tried using a copper metallic base here in the foyer but quickly realized that on such a large scale, the metallic copper "ghosting" through was simply too contemporary-looking for this old home. Here, the dramatic verdigris paint finish adds remarkable depth and convincing patina to the walls.

The trim color used throughout the house is Tatami Tan, a Sherwin Williams color. I prefer using old-fashioned, oil-based semi-gloss finish for trim work; it's both beautiful and durable.

23

Enrich the Atmosphere:

ADDING DECORATIVE EMBELLISHMENTS

There are hundreds of resources available for reproducing any style of specialty trim or molding imaginable. A simple search on the Internet will reveal thousands of products, from expensive hand-carved wood, to much less costly cast polyurethane. Although finding the exact style of decoration may take a little effort, the sense of historic character it adds is significant. Adding these embellishments was instrumental in unifying the décor of this three-story home; the trims and moldings create a transitional path from one room to the next that the eye can follow.

Think of adding period embellishments like ceiling medallions, chair railings, crown molding, recessed niches and cast resin ornamentation as if you were accessorizing a glamorous ballroom gown. In other words, choose ornamentation whose style, pattern and texture will not compete with the existing bones or architectural details in the space (like the grand staircase here in the foyer, for example), but instead complement the surroundings, like fine jewelry does for an evening gown. As you travel through the home, you'll notice how the subtle carvings on the moldings are echoed in the fabrics, wall treatments, stained-glass patterns, area rugs, accessories and even dishes. This ornate detail supplies the home with much of its subtle Gothic and Victorian flavor.

MATERIALS LIST

2-inch (51mm) chip brush, a selection of ¼-inch (6mm) to 1-inch (25mm) flat bristle brushes; "Minwax" Provincial #211 wood stain; rag; mineral spirits

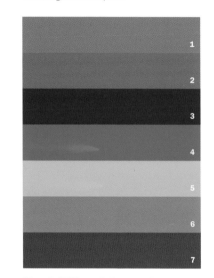

Sherwin Williams Palette: 1. Tatami Tan 2. Knockout Orange 3. Shamrock 4. Paradise 5. Bee 6. Navel 7. Copper Mountain

3 Antique the detailing. Working in sections, coat the molding with an oil wood stain (I used a dark walnut tone). Immediately after applying the stain, use a soft cloth moistened with mineral spirits to gently wipe stain from the carving. This will leave an aged-looking stain in the crevices that will simultaneously tone down the applied colors and soften the sculpted edges. Reapply as needed.
When all of the ornamentation has been antiqued and the stain is dry, you can apply a coat of satin polyurethane to even out the overall sheen and to protect the painted surface. (Some wood stains have sealant built in; check before applying more.)

1 Basecoat the embellishment. Using a 2-inch (51mm) chip brush, paint the ornamentation with a coat of tan semigloss oil paint. (Semigloss has an unsurpassed protective hardness and leaves behind a mellow finish that is ideal for older homes; the glossiness also works well when applying any type of faux finish atop.)

2 Drybrush the details. Using variously sized artist brushes, "pick out" the detail by drybrushing color on the raised decoration. The idea is to quickly deposit a dusting of pure color on specific portions of the decoration. I like to work from light to dark, starting with yellow, then proceeding with light orange, orange, lime green and darker green.

1. A Flexible Finish. The finishing technique demonstrated on these pages was loosely adapted for the curved stairwell ornamentation, ceiling medallion, and crown molding. Though similar in look and feel, each ornament varies in colors used and degree of drybrushing employed for highlighting detail. **2. Chandelier Medallion.** Looking up, you'll see the foyer chandelier emitting a wonderful glow on a classically designed, hand-painted floral medallion. You'd never suspect that the medallion is made of lightweight cast polyurethane, nor that the patina of age is brand new! **3. Crown Molding.** The crown molding draws the eye around the long, narrow entry hall. The ebonied molding emphasizes the length of the passageway. There's an occasional fine detail in this simple crown, which I made sure to place over the parlor and dining room entrances. **4. Chair Guard Molding.** Framing the beautiful Lincrusta® wainscoting, the chair guard molding (made of cast polyurethane) adds colorful detail. Its pattern is reminiscent of the swirling acanthus mural in the gathering room.

TORN-TISSUE FINISH

As a visitor's first and last impression of your home, the foyer should be a warm and inviting area. The foyer should also offer a preview of the rest of the house. In areas like the foyer, I prefer to use bold wall solutions like murals, richly patterned wallpaper or vibrant color. Murals work well because the varied palette gives you a lot of flexibility with which colors you can draw upon for other rooms. Murals, however, require good lighting and sufficient distance for viewing—and the foyer had neither of these characteristics. Instead, I decided to saturate the cavernous space with a torn tissue faux finish; this finish has a rich texture, and the amber-hued tones liven up the dark space. Paler variations of the amber color reappear throughout the house.

The torn-tissue finish is extremely simple to apply. Its characteristic crinkled appearance will add interesting texture to any room. One great advantage of this finish, I've discovered, is that there's virtually no need to prepare the wall prior to application. The tissue will cover nail holes, hairline cracks, small gouges, underlying wall color and a multitude of other sins!

MATERIALS LIST

Tissue paper; Floetrol paint additive; paint pan and roller; blue painter's tape; Modern Masters Latex Metallic Paint, no. ME-204 Antique Bronze; large drywall putty knife; 2-inch (51mm) chip brush; rags or cheesecloth

Sherwin Williams Palette: 1. Goldenrod

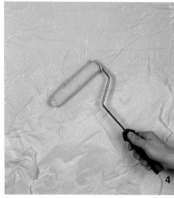

1 Prepare the main ingredients. Tape off all the moldings and trim prior to beginning. You'll need to tear the tissue paper in two different ways. One pile of tissue paper should be torn along all four edges. The other pile should be torn only along three sides, leaving one side straight and the three torn sides ragged. The straight edge will be essential for lining up along the ceiling, corners and baseboard edges.

2 Apply paint. Starting at the top of the wall by the ceiling, roll a heavy coat of the base onto a 4' × 4' (1m × 1m) area.

3 Immediately apply tissue. Immediately take a sheet of the tissue with the single straight edge and align that edge with the ceiling line. Allow the paper to "fall down" gently onto the wet surface so it adheres to the wet paint. *Do not* try to smooth it out! The object is to create a balanced, crinkled texture around the room. Continue applying tissue until the wet paint is covered.

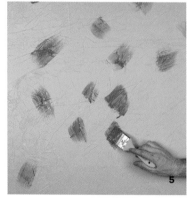

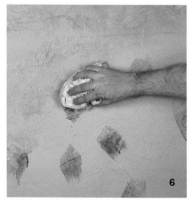

4 Apply second coat. Immediately after applying the tissue paper, roll on a second coat of the base color. Be very gentle as you apply this layer; you want to preserve the crinkled texture of the tissue paper. The tissue will be permanently sealed between the two coats of paint. While applying the second coat, roll on the first coat of the adjacent section. Apply tissue paper, apply second coat and move on to the next area. A rhythm will quickly emerge.

5 Color wash or glaze. To add an aged patina or to soften the tone, create a mixture of 1 part Floetrol paint additive and 1 part bronze-tinted latex glaze. Using a 2-inch (51mm) chip brush, randomly dab the mixture on the walls about six inches (15cm) apart, working in an area about 4' × 4' (1m × 1m) for manageability.

6 Blend the glaze. Immediately blend the paint with a damp rag. I added heavier tone around the corners, ceiling and baseboard edges for a stronger antiqued effect.

A Little Help From Your Friends. As with most faux finishes, having a second pair of hands will speed up the process. My friend and fellow decorative painter, Robin Harrison, assisted me in applying the torn tissue wall finish.

Notice the attention to detail on the original woodwork, including carving and fluting. Details like these are rare in the trim features found in today's architecture.

The Torn Tissue Finish. The crinkling texture and deep amber color add vibrancy to the otherwise dark corners of the foyer. The bronze metallic glaze adds depth and years of age to the edges.

HOW MUCH IS ENOUGH?

Purchase enough paint for two coats and enough tissue paper to cover the total square footage of the room. I used 20" × 30" (50cm × 75cm) sheets, purchased from a local wholesale paper supplier.

FANTASY-MARBLED PANELS

Fantasy marbling isn't intended to be a realistic impression of precious marble, so much as a somewhat whimsical interpretation. It's a type of marbling I enjoy because it has an almost "folk art" appearance. It's also a great way to emphasize particular colors in a space. In the foyer, the painted marble panels not only blend with the stained-glass window in the landing, but they also echo the rich ambers, aqua greens and blues, and terra cottas found throughout the house.

The long, narrow panels are accented with ornately carved trim. The colorful, busy pattern of the faux marble is soothed by the broad panels of bronzed mirror.

I was amazed by the variety of mirroring available: rose, peach, smoke, crackled, and even textured with marble-like gold veining! I finally selected a mellow, bronze-tinted mirror. Its warm, almost dusty reflection has an antique presence.

MATERIALS LIST

2-inch (51mm) chip brush; pin-striping brush; rags; spray bottle; softening brush; paint pan; sponge roller; soft-haired artist's brushes; optional oil glaze medium—oil tint and mineral spirits mixture, or polyurethane

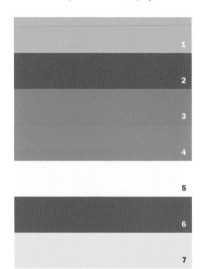

Sherwin Williams Palette: 1. Goldenrod 2. Copper Mountain 3. Knockout Orange 4. Chamois 5. Antique White 6. Derbyshire 7. June Day

1 **Basecoat the panels.** Prepare the walls, sanding them to be as smooth as possible to resemble real marble. Roll on a yellow basecoat with a satin finish.

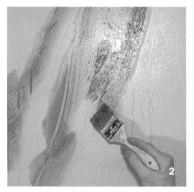

2 **Block in pattern.** The goal in this step is to define the pattern direction of your marble. Lightly mist a 4' × 4' (1m × 1m) working area. Load a 2-inch (51mm) chip brush with the colors of your choice. Streak the brush diagonally across the panel, skipping areas to let the base color show through.

3 **Add more texture.** Occasionally hit the wet areas with a crumpled rag to add additional texture. Keep in mind that these are the secondary colors; in the final stages these will only peek out from underneath. Work fairly quickly so you can blend the still-wet edge of the previous section with a new area.

4 **Feather the color.** Mist lightly here or there, then feather gently with a large, soft brush to fill in the gaps.

5 **Add primary color and pattern.** When the surface is dry, repeat steps 2 and 3 to apply the second range of colors. Choose colors that will complement the surrounding areas; here, I used Copper Mountain, Chamois and Knockout Orange. Let the colors bleed together as you apply them, either by double loading or allowing them to mix a little in the paint pan. Apply the colors randomly over the previous layer. It's important to apply the paint and then feather the colors in the same diagonal direction. Aim to create a balanced overall field of color.

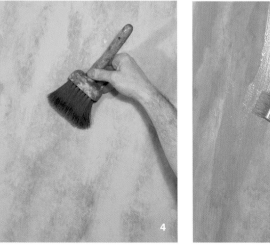

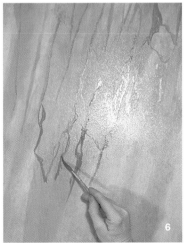

6 **Apply veining.** Veins in the marble can be applied with various tools, from pin striping brushes to actual feathers. I prefer striping brushes, which hold a nice amount of paint and allow for quick and fluid formation of veins. Dip the brush in water, blot it lightly on a rag, then dip it into the veining color. Starting at the top, bring the brush down with a squiggling motion that follows the diagonal direction. Outline the varied shapes and patterns of the underlayers.

7 **Define interesting shapes and colors.** Marbling can be as simple or complex as you choose. Here, I've taken it a step further by selectively filling in shapes with thinned color. This is a great way to emphasize the direction of the marble. Apply the paint, then immediately soften it with a badger or feathering brush.

8 **Glaze the marble.** To add a little more dimension, apply an oil glaze. Create a mixture of 3 parts oil glaze medium and 1 part mineral spirits. I tinted my glaze with oil based paint (June Day), adding a little color at a time, always thoroughly mixing, then testing the strength of the glaze on the marble panel. When the glaze has the right color and translucency, apply it with a sponge roller. Don't overload the roller—in fact, roll out the excess on a rag before applying the paint to the panel. Distribute the glaze evenly across the entire panel. A little bit of glaze goes a long, long way! If you don't wish to glaze the marble panel, simply roll a coat of polyurethane over the surface to seal the finish and even out the overall sheen.

The Secrets of Fine Marbling. The secret to fine marbling is making sure every vein line has a starting point and stopping point. Never leave a floating vein. This rarely occurs in real marble. For added realism, include veining going in the opposite diagonal, but don't overdo it. Occasionally spritz the field to help feather the vein lines, but don't allow runs to form.

PARLOR

A S YOU PASS THROUGH the ornately trimmed, open passageway from the foyer, you enter the parlor. The room has a formal yet charismatic charm about it. It is furnished with an eclectic mix of comfortable, plush upholstered furniture and antique side tables and accessories. The rustic cast iron garden table (now serving as a coffee table), with its weathered concrete top, nestles in front of the fringed, velvet brocade sofa. Odd marriages like this exemplify the house's often unexpected combination of raw materials.

Parlor Before. (Above) The parlor is the only room in the house that retains its original plastered walls. Layers of old, nicotine-stained wallpaper were removed and the settling cracks hiding beneath were painstakingly repaired.

The highlight of the space is the massive "bumped-out" fireplace. The new faux limestone mantel is matched with an intricate, hand-assembled, stained-glass mosaic surround. The mantel is anchored with a concrete hearth that is stamped and stained for a natural-looking stone texture. Instead of the usual mirror above the mantel, I've used this space to display my prized collection of Italian gilded wood sconces and English lusterware. The reflective gold, bronze, silver and copper surfaces sparkle against the faux-linen wall finish.

Parlor After. (At right) The room has a distinguished, opulent charm that sets a dignified tone for the house. The lushness of the decor and the elegance of the faux finishing create a sense of antiquity, transforming the barren front room into an inviting and intimate parlor.

Details Define the Setting

Artwork. To the left of the fireplace is a pair of antique, hand-colored etchings that depict opulent settings quite similar to this room.

Fabric. The golden tone-on-tone cotton damask print used for the window dressings filters the sunlight and produces a warm glow that floods the room.

Rug. The exotic, bold pattern and colors of the area rug contrasts brilliantly with the hand-painted walls and cherry-toned flooring.

Trim. The ebonized moulding with its Della Robbia accents provides a bold frame for the room and a perfect emphasis for the ten-foot ceilings. It is often mistaken for an original feature of the house. You'll notice how black is repeatedly used as a bold accent color—it appears throughout the house in picture frames, fireplace surrounds, and so on.

TROMPE L'OEIL CARVED LIMESTONE

Every room should have a focal point—that central item that immediately draws your eye and pulls you into the room. It can be just about anything—a stained-glass window or ornately patterned area rug, a colorful wall mural or a spotlighted sculpture. In the parlor, the fireplace acts as a commanding focal point. Not only does it jut out from the wall, but its central position directly across from the passageway makes it the first thing your eye encounters.

I decided to capitalize on this. For a European influence, I installed this massive, faux-limestone mantel. I discovered it while looking for a cost-efficient alternative to real limestone through a company called Mission Stone. The company offers a variety of legs and mantel ledges to choose from, allowing you to customize to a great degree. I decided to further enhance the stone appearance with trompe l'oeil limestone blocks—complete with grout lines—and carved decorations. It's fun to observe as guests run their hands across the mantel ledge in disbelief of the painted illusion. Oh, the joy of decorative painting!

RESOURCES

Mission Stone
1855 Hormel
San Antonio TX 78219
Phone: 1-866-678-6631
Website: www.missionstone.com

MATERIALS LIST

2-inch (51mm) chip brush; painter's tape; a selection of round artist's brushes; Behlen, Jet Spray toner in Raw Umber no. B101-0817; tracing paper; pencil; graphite transfer paper; candle; water spray bottle; rags

Sherwin Williams Palette: 1. Sands of Time 2. Java 3. Black of Night 4. Dover White

1 Tape off the grout lines and transfer the pattern. To make the mantel look as if it's composed of several limestone blocks, tear the edges of ½-inch blue painter's tape to form irregular edges and use this to define the individual blocks. Keep in mind that you want fairly large blocks when you place the tape strips.

Once your design is complete, sketch half of it (to scale) onto tracing paper. Slip graphite paper beneath it and transfer the design to the right half of the mantel. Flip the design over so it is the mirror image, slip graphite paper beneath, then transfer the drawing to the left side.

2 Paint the trompe l'oeil. To give the illusion of hand-carved stone, use three tones: a medium body tone (Sands of Time), a shadow tone (Java) and a highlight accent (Dover White), plus black. Lay in part of the design with the body tone, quickly rinse your brush, then follow behind with the shadow tone. Leave it heavy at the bottom then feather out into the body color. Rinse the brush again, and follow up with a strong highlight on the opposite side, again slightly blending it into the body tone. As you paint, take your cue from any natural light sources entering the room; make sure your shadows and highlights fall accordingly.

3 Age the blocks. This step can be completed prior to painting the carved details, but I find it adds more believability if done afterwards. Either way, cover the surrounding areas and make sure the room is adequately ventilated, then lightly spray a "halo" along the perimeter of each stone block with the wood toner spray. Use a light touch with the spray, letting it feather out toward the center of each block.

4 **Soften the toner.** Soften the obvious spray effect by stippling. Spritz the block with water, load a 2-inch (51mm) chip brush with the body tone from the previous step, and pounce it across the block, especially over the sprayed areas. This will add a blemished and pitted texture to the finish. Use a damp rag to mottle the stippled effect.

5 **Remove the grout tape and add soot.** Slowly remove the grout tape. Using the three tones from step 2, shade and highlight the edges (paying attention to the source of natural light) to complete the illusion. For an extra bit of "instant aging," hold a lit candle at an angle beneath the mantle's edge, allowing the flame to blacken the edge of the mantel. The black smoke effect adds incredible realism. To prevent the black soot from rubbing off, seal with polyurethane spray. Finally, brush a coat of low-luster polyurethane over the entire mantel to seal and even out the painted finish.

A Grand Presence. (Right) The completed fireplace now has a grand presence in the room. Dissecting the mantel ledge into three limestone blocks gave it a feeling of substance and weight. The "carved" design echoes the laurel wreath pattern in the stenciled wall finish. The center rosette is a stylized version of the floral motif found in the stained-glass-mosaic surround, the area rug, and elsewhere throughout the home.

TIME SPENT ON THE JOB

Hand-painted details take most of my time on a job. All-over aging is often just a matter of a spray or quickly applied toner (I love getting so much accomplished with one step!), but hand-painted details can't be rushed.

To create a more formal feel in the front parlor, I applied a lavish, faux linen-damask finish. I maintained the warm amber Tuscan color palette used throughout the main floor, using a beautiful golden strié over the elaborate pattern and rich terra-cotta basetone (Roycraft Copper Red); this imitates the fine threads that are characteristic of raw silk or linen. Although this finish appears complex, it comes to life with little more than basic stenciling, ragging and strié painting techniques.

MATERIALS LIST

Stencil (posterboard); craft knife; spray paint; blue painter's tape; tape measure; pencil; spray adhesive (3M Super 77); gold metallic spray paint; dust masks; round artist's brushes; Easy Mask "KleenEdge" tape; cotton rags, water; mineral spirits; empty gallon paint can or mixing container; Sherwin Williams Illusions Glazing Liquid; spray bottle; strié brush; 2-inch (51mm) chip brush; sponge roller; paint pan

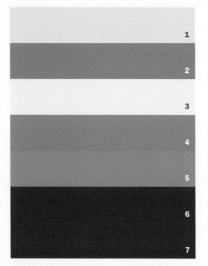

Sherwin Williams Palette: 1. June Day 2. Cut the Mustard 3. Inviting Ivory 4. Butter Scotch 5. Tatami Tan 6. Roycroft Copper Red 7. Terra Brun

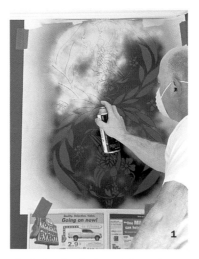

1 **Determine the layout.** Determine the layout of the pattern, then make guide marks around the room with a pencil. Prepare your stencil, and spray the back of it with adhesive to secure it to the wall. Starting at the top of the wall, position the stencil using a couple pieces of blue painter's tape for extra adhesion. Transfer the pattern by spraying through the stencil with a gold metallic paint. Remove and reposition the stencil, working down the wall and around the room.

2 **Detail the pattern.** To add dimension to the design and to further the illusion of hand-printed damask fabric, shade the laurel wreath using three tones: a medium (Cut the Mustard), dark (Terra Brun) for shadowing, and a light (Inviting Ivory) for highlighting. Using a round artist brush that holds a nice amount of paint, apply the medium color. Lay the tone in a rapid, fluid stroke that follows the contours of the stencil pattern. Make sure you allow the gold to show through. Follow with the ivory highlight and finish with a defining stroke of brown.

3 **"Rag" the panels.** Mask the stripes using low-tack white tape. To add a warm mottled tone to the background, bunch up a damp cotton cloth in your hand and dab it into the Cut the Mustard. Remove any excess paint and then "rag" the wall. I find it helps to have a spray bottle nearby to occasionally spritz the rag and paint pan, so the color stays soft and fluid. The aim here is to give the fabric panels a slightly patinated look. Carefully peel away the tape to reveal the red stripes.

4 **Glaze the walls.** Create a mixture of about three parts oil glaze and one part mineral spirits. Add a little bit of oil color (June Day + Cut the Mustard) at a time, slowly building the translucent glaze. For a strié glaze, the mixture should have the consistency of motor oil. If it's too thick, add more mineral spirits. If it needs to be more opaque, add more paint.

5 **Strié the walls.** While the glaze is still wet, strié the panel. Start at the top and slowly drag a strié brush down the wall. Avoid stopping; try to strié the wall in one graceful sweep. You probably won't reach the bottom comfortably, so stop as close to the base as possible. Position the brush at the base and strié upwards, blending into the previous striations. Occasionally wipe the brush with a mineral spirit-soaked rag. Don't worry about making your strié lines perfectly straight. Irregular "squiggles" are desirable, as long as the lines have an overall parallel feel.

Building Up the Entryway. (Right) Open entrances, like the one shown here, are perfect areas for easily and affordably adding "period" architectural interest. I built up this ordinary passageway by adding raised, fluted pilasters, Corinthian capitals, a crown-molded lintel and a centered keystone. Decorative moldings and trims are easily available and come in a vast array of styles to suit any environment. Emphasizing an entryway is a simple and inexpensive way to add historical charm to any setting.

Decisions, Decision, Decisions. (Below) I'm easily bored by stale environments, so I find myself moving furniture and accessories around a lot. (You'll notice this if you look closely at the photographs in this book: certain items just seem to wander from one floor to the next.) The two photos here show the same corner during photoshoots months apart. I tried the garden statues first; the well-seasoned patina seemed striking against the rich faux finish. A few months later, I found myself switching them out with the plush chair and delicate side table. When making furniture and other home décor choices, keep in mind that coordinating fabrics, patterns and textures will make it easier to use a piece in different settings. If you have the flexibility to do it, shifting furniture can be a very cost effective way to reinvent a room.

ANTIQUED CROWN MOLDING

As you saw in the foyer, lavishly carved trims and moldings can add significant architectural interest to a room. You can use these elements to direct the eye from one space to the next and to create a continuity throughout the home. In my quest to introduce an Italianate flavor to the fixed architectural details, I searched for items with classically Italian representation; the delicate Della Robbia flowers and ribbon design on this crown molding, edged with a classic egg and dart detail, is a perfect example.

I chose to finish the crown molding with a Biedermeier-like ebony finish, similar to the finish on the foyer's grand staircase. Here in the parlor, the rich, contrasting finish of the crown molding adds a visual weight, forcing your eye around the ceiling line. The molding is indeed the crowning touch to this lavish living area.

MATERIALS LIST

2-inch (51mm) chip brush; old trim brush; rags

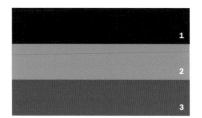

Sherwin Williams Palette: 1. Black of Night 2. Goldcrest 3. Copper Mountain

1 **Basecoat the molding.** After taping off the crown, paint the entire molding by heavily stippling on a single coat of Acrylic Black Enamel with an old soft trim brush.

2 **Drybrush the molding.** Using a 2-inch (51mm) chip brush, lightly drybrush the entire molding with latex satin paint. Load the brush first with the darker orange shade (Copper Mountain), dabbing off the excess on a paper towel or rag. Using a feather-light touch, drybrush quickly across all of the raised detail areas, one 3-foot (1m) section at a time.

3 **Add a soft dusting of color.** When the brush is nearly bare of paint, "swoosh" what is left under and around the edges of the detail to add a soft dusting of color. Continue to drybrush the detail, layering and building up the density of color.

4 **Highlight the molding.** Load a 2-inch (51mm) chip brush with the lighter yellow shade (Goldcrest). Drybrush the upper portions of the raised areas. Continue until the color is balanced, then move to the next section until the entire crown is complete. Once you develop a rhythm, you'll discover that drybrushing is a quick and simple way to create a natural-looking, aged patina.

Molding in its Original Form. The crown molding is made of high-density, foam polyurethane. This material is perfect for faux paint finishes; the raised decoration is very pronounced, and there are deep recesses and gullies for the paint to seep into, suggesting years of dust and soot accumulation. This product is also light-weight (making it easy to install), easy to cut and crack-resistant.

Della Robbia. Inspiration can be derived from the simplest objects. Discovered at an estate sale, this dainty soup tureen with its whimsical cherubs and lush Della Robbia decoration motivated my choice of crown molding.

CUSTOM-MADE, STAINED-GLASS MOSAIC SURROUND

When renovating a historic home, keep any new, permanent fixtures in tune with the house. Moldings, cabinets, flooring, chandeliers and wall sconces, plumbing fixtures and fireplace "dressings" should all appear organic to the house. In this case, I needed to match the late-1800s feel of the house.

The fireplaces were a challenge. The outside chimneys had to be partially rebuilt, tuck pointed, and capped; the collapsed interior chimney had to be reopened and cleared of debris, then relined; the fireboxes had to be rebuilt and refitted for new gas lines; and the hearths had to be repoured with concrete, then stamped and stained. It was a lot of effort, but having four safe and working fireplaces in a home that's over one hundred years old has proved to be a great benefit to the house's value, ambiance and character. Customizing the fireplaces with mantels and tiled surrounds added timeless appeal to the individual rooms.

Here in the parlor, for example, the custom mosaic surround boldly anchors the massive faux limestone mantel. The delicate, glittering colors have an undeniable allure. A local tile specialist and artist, Pete Crable, meticulously constructed the surround from hundreds of tiny glass tiles. His painstaking work resulted in a permanent fixture that is not only original, but also appears to be original to the house!

The Artist at Work. (Above) Mosaic artist Pete Crable carefully selects and positions each individual tile, adding depth and volume to the design. Notice that the tiles are separated into piles by color and intensity. Arranging the tiles in this way significantly lessens your frustration later as you assemble the colossal puzzle.

Detail of the Assembly Process. To ensure a snug fit, Crable employs tile nippers to cut and shape the tiny glass pieces.

Mantel Surround Detail. The gradation of value in the ribbon gives it a strong sense of movement and depth.

Mantel Surround. The one-of-a-kind mosaic surround is truly an original work of art. The intricate shading and highlighting on the spiraling ribbon (a motif borrowed from the foyer's transom window), adds depth and a flowing movement to the piece. The intense cobalt flowers, rich terra-cotta ribbon and butter-shaded borders seem to float against the sparkling ebony background. If the limestone hadn't been "dirtied" with the aged patina, its lightness would have contrasted too intensely with the dark colors of the surround; as it is, the relationship between the soft, aged mantel and sharp, glittering surround is remarkably balanced.

The Floral Thread

Any visitor with a keen eye will see the subtle floral thread that's woven throughout the house. Stylized variations of the motif take bloom in carved furniture, area rugs, printed fabrics, hand-made tiles, stained glass windows, cabinets, hardware and so on.

Artists have always relied on flowers as a source of inspiration; it's a classic theme with a universal pull. Our spirits are lifted by the first sighting of a timid crocus pushing through the frozen earth, and with each blooming flower that follows through the seasons. Why wouldn't we want to carry that joyful color and beauty into our homes?

1. **Guest Room.** A detail from the cast iron border on the fireplace surround. **2. Guest Room.** A detail from the trumeau mirror. **3. Parlor.** A detail from a cast iron side table. **4. Parlor.** A detail from the carved cupboard. **5. Second Floor Hallway.** A carved detail from an antique secretary. **6. Parlor.** A detail from the carving along a mirror. **7. Parlor.** A mosaic detail from the fireplace surround. **8. Parlor.** A detail from the area rug.

5

6

7

8

DINING ROOM

A PROFUSION OF NATURAL LIGHT spills from the leaded, stained glass window that dominates the outside wall. Decorative art flourishes in this space, as the walls, ceiling and mantel set the stage for a memorable atmosphere that's perfectly dressed for entertaining.

As a centrally located room in the original floor plan of the house, the dining room had to be more than a "pass-through" room. I added several architectural features to accomplish this, like the raised paneling, stained glass, built-in serving consoles, and the arched passageways to the foyer and kitchen. Once I discovered it, I reopened the closed-off fireplace, which went a long way to making the room into a perfect gathering place for family and friends.

Watercolor Rendition. I often paint watercolor renditions of my ideas to scale. This helps me—and my clients—visualize the outcome. I make certain departures, but this is an excellent tool for planning the décor.

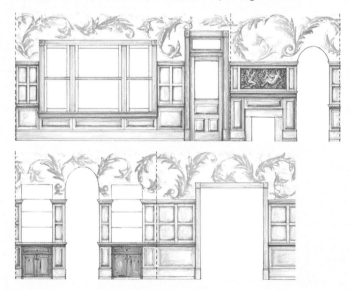

Where Family and Friends Gather. (Right) Ready for guests, the beautifully set dining table elegantly furnishes the comfortable room. Replacing the traditional china cabinet, a plate ledge showcasing fancifully colored Italian plates circles the room.

Details Define the Setting

Arched symmetry. The arched entrance is a new addition to the space. It was rebuilt, according to evidence found under layers of old linoleum and shag carpet, as close to the original location as possible. I arched the passageway as discussed earlier, to reinforce the Gothic influence I was trying to add to the home.

Acanthus pattern. For warmth, I applied a lyrical, oversized frieze above the paneling. The raised dimensions of the meandering acanthus add visual interest for seated guests. The frieze's distressed-looking, playful appearance helps relax the atmosphere of the room.

Harmonious palette. Rich ambers and olive greens combine with terra cotta accents to balance the room. A softer version of this palette can be seen in the kitchen mural through the passageway. A unified palette is extremely important in a house with an open floor plan.

THE CURVED WINDOW

One of the most attractive features of the house is the magnificent curved window in the dining room. In making this house my home, I invested a lot in replacing the old, damaged glass with a custom-made, stained-glass window. This work of art was designed in collaboration with Ohio stained glass artisan, Dave Ehrnschwender.

This project presented several obstacles. The primary obstacle was also one of the window's most attractive features: its curved shape. The artist assembled custom-arched bed forms—one concave and the other convex—on which he painstakingly arranged the glass pieces. To preserve as much of the house's history as possible, he recycled most of the surviving glass in the new design. The old glass was cut into various sizes, joined with new, colorful stained glass, then leaded and aged to suggest that it had been here forever. The results are breathtaking!

The Window Before. The old, wavy and pitted curved glass was either cracked beyond repair or missing altogether (part of the center window had actually been outfitted with Plexiglas). Notice how the dropped ceiling covered the upper portion of the original molding. Previous owners had nailed the ceiling frame into the wood with 3-inch nails (75mm), almost damaging the beautiful original moldings beyond repair.

The Window After. The magnificent window sets the tone for this home, reinforcing the Gothic features of both the interior and exterior. The unexpected jewel-like shades of cobalt, ruby, emerald and amber are repeated around the room in the hand-painted china decorating the old-fashioned plate ledge. The southern exposure makes for a lovely morning welcome.

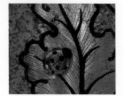

Details from Stained Glass. These details fill the border. Some, like the ladybug, are actually three dimensional.

ITALIAN CERAMICS

My favorite collection of hand-made Italian ceramics decorates the plate ledge and dining room table. The jubilant colors, characteristic of Italian pottery, add unexpected energy to the room. Being able to change the pieces along the ledge to suit the season or event has been a wonderful benefit of the plate ledge.

The beautiful round table and Windsor chairs were generously on loan from my dear friend, Jeff. The ones that I ordered were to have been delivered on time for the photoshoot, but were nowhere in sight!

FAUX-FRESCO FRIEZE

Dining room décor should always offer the sitting guest something interesting to look at, be it framed artwork or a custom, full-room mural. This dining room incorporates several layers of visual excitement, including the paneled walls with their plate ledge of colorful china, the fresco-like frieze above it, and the vibrant starburst medallion on the ceiling. Add those to the wall of stained-glass windows and the mantel with its Italianate panel, and you'll find no view unworthy of a guest's attention.

A frieze is decoration specifically designed for the horizontal upper portions of a wall. Traditionally, it's a raised embellishment with shadows and reflective qualities that add dimension to the area. I gave this frieze dimension by using joint compound and paint. To further the illusion, I lightly distressed and antiqued the surface to resemble a fresco. A real fresco requires the tedious task of painting onto wet plaster. This quick faux version is much more forgiving and fun to experiment with, especially for beginners.

MATERIALS LIST

All-purpose joint compound; 12-inch (30cm) steel taping knife; 6-inch (15cm) and 1 ½-inch (37mm) flexible putty knives; ¾-inch (19mm) nap roller; sponge roller; oil-based glaze; 2-inch (51mm) chip brush; spray bottle; 100-grit sand paper; rag; chalk

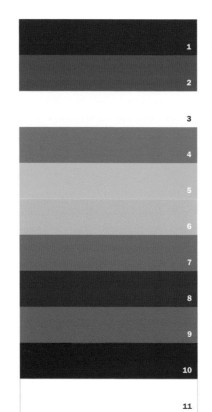

Sherwin Williams Palette: 1. Java 2. Rosemary 3. Full Moon 4. Cut the Mustard 5. Anjou Pear 6. Clary Sage 7. Artichoke 8. Rookwood Dark Green 9. Decorous Amber 10. Rock Garden 11. Corona

1 Texture the background. To create an even backdrop for the frieze, place a working amount of compound onto a 12-inch (30cm) steel taping knife. Load a 6-inch (15cm) flexible putty knife with about a ¼-inch (6mm) bead of compound; then, starting at the ceiling edge, lightly "skip" the compound down the wall in various directions. Occasionally leave bits of bare wall exposed. Gently feather out each application while still wet by floating the almost-clean blade over these areas. For best results, work as quickly and loosely as possible when applying the texture until the walls are uniformly textured. Let dry.

2 Transfer the pattern. Sketch the acanthus pattern directly onto the wall, with chalk or pastel. Use your scaled rendering as a guide only, and be ready to adapt your design for architectural elements like corners, switch plates and air vents. Be most critical at the corners; make sure the design transitions naturally from one plane to the next. Step down from the ladder regularly to check your progress. Move about the room to view the design from different vantage points.

WHERE TO START

Begin any decorative paint project on the wall least noticeable from the room's entrance. This allows you the time to figure out any technique problems, which hopefully will be quickly solved as you move around the room.

4 **Seal the bare drywall compound.** When the walls are completely dry, apply a neutral, latex satin basecoat (I used Antique White) to seal the raw joint compound and to prepare the surface for decorative painting. Use a ¾-inch (19mm) nap roller to apply the basecoat so the paint will seep into the textured crevices. The basecoat will seal the joint compound and even out the tone, making a good surface for the detail painting and color washing that follows.

5 **Color wash the entire mural.** A color wash is a simple paint finish that adds instant warmth to a plain-colored surface. Start by choosing one to four paint colors (you should only need a quart of each), making sure they have a satin or eggshell base so the paint glides across the surface. Mist an area of the wall—about 4' × 4' (1m × 1m)—with water, then dab a 2-inch (51mm) chip brush into one or two colors, picking up a tiny amount of paint. Randomly scrub the paint into the misted wall area, feathering the paint into the adjacent areas.

3 **Sculpt the relief.** Following the outline of the pattern, begin sculpting the design using the 1 ½-inch (37mm) flexible putty knife. Place about 3 cups (711ml) of joint compound into the mud pan, then tint it with a spoonful of yellow latex paint. This will make it easier to see the pattern as you apply it over the textured background. Load about a ¼-inch (6mm) bead of the compound onto the 1 ½-inch (37mm) flexible putty knife, and deposit the heaviest bead on the top and bottom edges of the outline, feathering out towards the center. Continue working around the outline until the pattern looks three-dimensional. Irregular edges are desirable, as is the background peeking through.

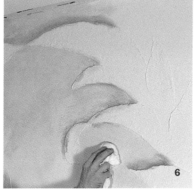

6 **Blend the colors.** Use a damp rag to spread the tone, blending the various colors. Once you've achieved a satisfying range of translucent, broken color, lightly dry-brush the area to eliminate any noticeable marks left by the brush or rag. Repeat, working across the wall and then down (so water runs don't disturb previous color-washed areas), until a unified range of broken color is achieved.

DRAWING ON WALLS

If you're not comfortable sketching directly onto the wall with chalk—even though any mistake can easily be removed with a damp cloth—then the design can be transferred in other ways, such as using an overhead projector. If you're truly interested in developing your skills as a decorative artist, however, try forcing yourself to draw directly onto the surface. Doing this will help sharpen your illustration skills and build your confidence at drawing in a large scale format. With some practice, a paint brush will replace the chalk in your hand. This will save valuable time for moving forward with the more important painting details!

47

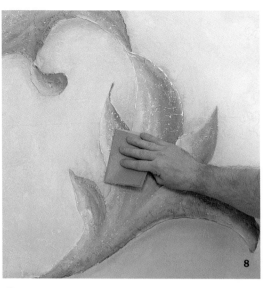

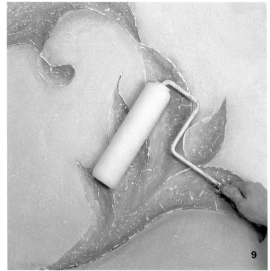

7 Paint the relief design. Using soft-bristled artist brushes—square-tipped or brights—paint the details. Add a variety of greens, along with an off-white (Antique White) and an umber (Java) to your palette. Load some of the medium green onto the brush, and establish a base tone for the leaf. Occasionally dip your brush in the water to help push the paint about. (This technique is very similar to watercolor painting.) While the base tone is still wet, blend the highlight and shadow areas according to how any natural light enters the room. Work quickly to blend the colors while they're still wet.

8 Distress the frieze. Using 100-grit sandpaper and a damp rag, gently sand the design's highlights and raised textures. Here and there, vigorously rub the wall surface with the damp rag to soften the scratches from the sandpaper. Distress the mural a little at a time, being attentive to areas where more natural aging would occur. Step back. Is the patina balanced around the room? You can reapply color with a quick wash if you went too far in areas.

If the white of the compound showing through seems harsh, simply color wash a light, somewhat dirty-looking tone over the frieze. This should soften the whites of the compound, and—as an added bonus—lightly seals the plaster. Add a little extra color under the raised, sanded areas and in the corners to suggest decades of natural aging.

9 Seal the mural. If you think the mural may need to be protected against wear and tear (e.g., little handprints or sprays of champagne), seal it with a thinned oil glaze rather than the more typical satin polyurethane. The oil glaze sheen is more mellow and appropriate for a faux fresco. Stir together a half gallon (2 liters) of one part glaze and one part mineral spirits. If you wish to tint the entire project, simply add a small amount of oil color or universal tint to the mixture. (Add color slowly; it's nearly impossible to lighten without wasting a lot of material and time.) Your final mixture should be the consistency of buttermilk. Using a mohair brush or sponge roller, spread the glaze as evenly as possible across the wall. Look down the wall from an angle to ensure that no areas have been skipped. The shiny surface will dry to a rich, eggshell glow overnight.

The Acanthus Pattern. The pattern for this frieze was derived from the acanthus flower, which is indigenous to the Mediterranean. Its fanciful leaves were commonly first used in stylized representation in Greek and Roman culture as early as the fifth century B.C, often symbolizing good health and longevity. Most commonly, the leaf was used as decoration on Corinthian capitals, topping classical Greek and Roman columns. If you look closely, modern interpretation of the leaf appears throughout this home's décor. I've always wanted to experiment with an oversized interpretation of the leaf, and the upper wall area in the dining room proved to be the perfect canvas. The rambling design, with its seductive curves and spirited motion, seems to energize the setting. The invigorating action of the frieze clashes with the otherwise relaxed tone of the room, making for a visually unforgettable dining experience!

The Feel of Fresco. This mural of rambling acanthus leaves is an attempt to capture the feel of fresco, a centuries-old technique of painting on wet plaster. Faux fresco technique is perfect for disguising crumbling plaster walls in older homes. Because it's painted on a rough, uneven surface and will be distressed, it's also the perfect technique for a beginning muralist. All it requires is some basic shading and highlighting techniques to create a beautiful work of art.

WATER-BASED PAINT

Any water-based paint can be used for this project, but I've found that latex satin house paint works great. It's not costly, lasts longer than acrylic tube paints and dries to a beautiful sheen. After buying paint, I transfer it to a clear squeeze bottle so I can clearly see the tone. I always label the container with the brand name and identification number so I can reconstruct what I did, if necessary.

TERRA-COTTA FAUX FINISH

During demolition, I discovered that a fireplace had once graced the dining room. Since I was trying to restore as much of the original architectural character of the home as possible, I decided to rebuild it.

My original design ideas involved placing a traditional beveled mirror in the center panel, but a visit to a favorite consignment shop yielded two Italian-inspired, vintage pressed-tin panels. The mirror became an unregretted memory. One panel fit the space perfectly, and has become a favorite conversation piece. The sister panel found its place in the kitchen's range hood.

The original finish on the pressed tin, while an attractive color, was harshly executed and was badly marred and rusted. Taking my cue from the color, I came up with an aged terra-cotta faux finish. This finish is simple to execute, and its warm and mellow patina is perfect for many surfaces, but especially those with raised detailing.

JOINT COMPOUND AND PAINT

Because joint compound is water-based, it can only be tinted with water-based products. Always use a tint stronger in hue than the color you are trying to achieve—the moisture already in the compound dramatically dilutes paint pigment.

MATERIALS LIST

Joint compound; 2-inch (51mm) chip brush; rags; oil glaze or polyurethane

Sherwin Williams Palette: 1. Inviting Ivory 2. Colonial Yellow 3. Marquis Orange 4. Constant Coral 5. Cajun Red

1 Base paint the object. For aged finishes, I like to use several colors for the base; it adds far more interest than a solid tone would. Apply shades of orange, rust and pink randomly, blending the colors with a 2-inch (51mm) chip brush. Try to keep the raised areas of your object lighter, and the crevices darker to suggest age.

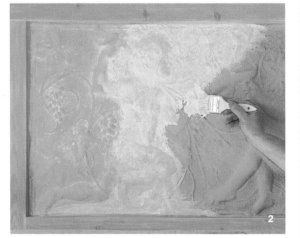

2 Apply a coat of chalky paint. To achieve the weathered look of terra-cotta, tint a workable amount (I used about a cup [237ml] here) of joint compound with a light yellow latex paint. (Tinting the mixture with white will turn the piece very pink). When you've achieved the right color, load a 2-inch (51mm) chip brush with the mixture. Working swiftly, stipple the mixture into the crevices and recessed areas. When this is complete, lightly drybrush the remaining areas, working the brush in different directions.

3 Distress the finish. When the compound mixture is completely dry, gently remove some of the mixture with a damp rag, leaving more mixture in the indentations and detail areas of the piece. The result is a faded, chalky dusting on the piece. To protect the surface, seal it with an oil-based glaze or polyurethane (*don't* use latex sealant—the water in this product will remove the water-based joint compound). Once the panel is sealed, you may want to stipple a moss green or burnt umber into the details for an even more convincing weathered patina.

During the Demolition. The fireplace had been totally closed off and hidden behind layers of old plaster, drywall and wood paneling.

After the Construction. The vintage panel fit the fireplace perfectly. I simply applied construction adhesive to the back and secured it with a couple of drywall screws.

The Completed Dining Room. (Left) The built-in mantel feels natural to the house. The decorative faux terra-cotta inset creates the whimsical tone I was striving for. Its playful design of entangled grapevines and cherubs celebrates the spirit that gathering with loved ones is all about. When I come across unusual discoveries, such as this tin panel, at antique markets or thrift shops, I rarely leave them behind (even if I haven't clue what will be done with them). When an *objet d'art* excites your imagination, your design sensibilities will find a home for it.

I completed the fireplace with sleek, black granite facing to accent the firebox. The copper flakes in the granite harmonized perfectly with the warm palette of the room. The cast iron trim of the surround was original, so I refitted it and cleaned up the egg-and-dart detailing with a drybrushed bronze patina.

RUSTIC, FAUX-PICKLED FINISH

Over the years, I've spent time observing and learning from the constantly fluctuating styles of interior design. I keep a journal in which I note the particular details of a memorable setting. Bits and pieces from this journal helped in the rebirth of this dining room.

For example, the idea for replacing the dark, 1960s paneling with warm pine was resurrected from a commission I completed years ago. Though that room was in a classic Georgian Colonial home, I felt that the intimacy of the paneled walls would fit any interior. The owners of the Georgian home had topped the paneling with a plate ledge where they displayed their cherished china collection, an idea that I couldn't resist borrowing.

I made the paneling less formal, choosing inexpensive pine plywood for the construction. I love how the exaggerated knots and graining of the pine stand out against the mellow glow of the pickled finish. The combined effect adds just the right amount of formal elegance to the room, balancing the jubilance of the acanthus frieze.

MATERIALS LIST

2-inch (51mm) chip brush; Sherwin Williams Wood Classics interior oil stain no. 3116 Honeytone; Minwax pre-stain; joint compound; oil-based glaze; orbital sander; 150-grit sandpaper; dust mask

Sherwin Williams Palette: 1. Friendly Yellow 2. Honeytone

1 **Seal the bare wood.** Before attempting to do any type of stained finish on bare wood, apply a coat of wood conditioner. I use Minwax pre-stain, which helps especially soft wood, like pine, absorb the stain more evenly.

2 **Apply stain.** For a warm, honey-pine color, apply a tinted stain (Honeytone) with a 2-inch (51mm) chip brush, almost scrubbing the stain into the grain. For a slightly aged appearance, apply a second coat more heavily along the inside edges of each panel.

3 **Apply pickling coat.** I wanted the finished paneling to look as if it had once been painted white, and then stripped, leaving behind bits of paint and grime in the wood grain. To do this, I mixed about a gallon (4 liters) of joint compound with 4 tablespoons (60ml) of yellow latex paint (Friendly Yellow). (Using joint compound instead of paint will create a chalkier look in the grainy crevices and textured knots.) The mixture should have the consistency of heavy pancake batter. Apply the mixture thickly with a 2-inch (51mm) chip brush over all of the paneling, scrubbing the mixture into the raised grain and recessed knots. Working in the direction of the grain, apply a second coat around the edges, where there would be a natural build-up of paint. Let the panels dry overnight.

4 **Distress the finish.** Before sanding, seal open doorways (to prevent dust from going into other rooms), open windows for ventilation, and put on a dust mask. Begin sanding off the compound mixture. For the large flat panels, I used an orbital sander, set on slow speed with 150-grit sandpaper. I sanded the corners and finer areas by hand. Where there would be an obvious build-up of paint, like corners and knots, sand more lightly. This will also smooth the roughness of the raw plywood. Try not to sand all the way to the honey-toned stain, as this will give the wood a pinkish cast.

5 **Seal with tinted glaze.** To further soften the graining and simultaneously seal the paneling, apply a thick coat of oil-based glaze. (*Do not* apply any water-based products, which will remove the joint compound mixture.) Make a glaze mixture of three parts oil-based glaze and one part mineral spirits. Slowly tint the mixture—a teaspoon (5ml) at a time—with white oil-based paint, until you're satisfied with the level of opacity. Using a 2-inch (51mm) chip brush, apply the glaze following the direction of the grain. For added protection (and to make the paneling easier to clean), add a final coat of satin polyurethane to the dried, sealed finish.

A Softened Effect. (Right) The pickled finish, dramatically softens the otherwise busy pattern of the unfinished pine paneling, but still allows for the exaggerated graining and occasional know to "ghost" through. The resulting finish adds an intimate, cozy feeling to the room, contrasting beautifully with the painted trim and frieze.

DIMENSIONAL STARBURST MEDALLION

To capture the sophistication and old-world ambiance of classic European interiors, walls, floors and even ceilings should be considered part of a collective whole when it comes to décor. Europeans love to embellish every surface, often using bold mixtures of materials, patterns, textures and colors. It is that enthusiasm for decoration that I find most attractive about the culture and that I have tried to capture here.

Borrowing from a starburst motif in the parlor area rug, I developed a stylized floral design for the ceiling. The hovering, tone-on-tone blossom dramatically transforms an otherwise dull and lifeless area.

Someday, I intend to add a tone-on-tone color wash to the remainder of the ceiling, softening the transition from the walls to the ceiling, but for now the frosted, peach-tinted glass globes of the chandelier cast a warm glow over the ceiling.

MATERIALS LIST

Several square-tipped artist brushes; overhead projector; paper; ballpoint pen; joint compound; water

Sherwin Williams Palette: 1. Enjoyable Yellow 2. Yarrow 3. Rookwood Medium Brown

1 **Transfer the pattern to the ceiling.** After designing the motif, I enlarged it to scale on paper using an overhead projector, then taped the paper to the ceiling. Once the paper was secure, I traced the lines of the pattern with a ballpoint pen, pressing hard enough to leave a dent in the drywall. The indentations are barely visible to the naked eye, but you can easily trace over them afterward with a pencil if necessary.

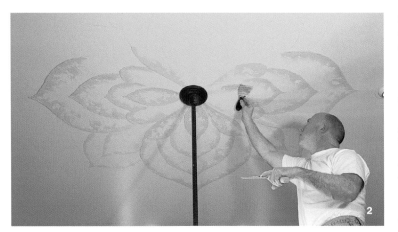

2 **Sculpt the pattern onto ceiling.** I decided to add further interest and dimension to the design by sculpting the individual petals of the starburst with joint compound. Mix a workable amount of compound with a few drops of yellow paint and form the design, following the indentations. Go around a couple of times, building up the depth of the center petals. Start by leaving a heavier bead at the edge of each petal, feathering the compound toward the center. To build up the center vein of some petals, place a thick line of compound down the center then feather this toward the outer edges.

3 **Paint the medallion.** After the compound has completely dried, begin painting, working from the center out. Basecoating first is an option, but it isn't necessary. Place a cup of water and several shades of yellow—a highlight tone, medium tone and shading tone—into the paint pan. Using basic shading techniques and square-edged artists brushes, lay in the colors until the desired look is achieved. To create a stronger patina, you can sand lightly after painting.

An Old-World Light. The mood is warmed by the glow from the antique, hand-carved wooden chandelier. I purchased this in pieces at an antiques fair, then rebuilt and rewired the piece. I brought the wood's luster back to life with several coats of beeswax. The delicate carvings on the arms resemble acanthus leaves, with tiny bunches of grapes attached. In addition, there are several recessed perimeter lights (highlighting the mantel decoration and stained glass windows), but the mood of the room is determined by this classic chandelier.

Inspiration. The inspiration for the ceiling frieze is borrowed from the starburst motif in the parlor area rug. The echo of designs and shapes throughout the house is a subtle, yet pleasing design effect.

KITCHEN

A S WITH MOST HOMES today, this kitchen truly serves as the "heart" of this home. Although it's small compared to modern construction standards, measuring just 11'9" × 14' (3.5m × 4.3m), the space is most functional, warm and inviting. I wanted to create an environment rich in color and texture, yet lighthearted in mood and overall atmosphere.

Decorative painting details flourish in the kitchen. The walls feature trompe l'oeil accents of broken plaster, exposed brick and wood laths. A meandering trail of ivy directs the eye around the room. An occasional bird or bug surprises the viewer. The decorative range hood—the companion to the panel in the dining room—features a lone grapevine-entangled cherub painted in vivid colors to resemble a time-worn fresco. Above the scene, three massive faux-wood-grained beams further define this kitchen inspired by a classic Italian country villa I visited once in Tuscany.

Kitchen After Construction. (Above) After the hardware was installed, the kitchen had a clean, comfortable feel, but it wasn't until the painting was complete that it felt like the "heart" of the house.

The Completed Kitchen. (Right) The warm tones of the kitchen match the house's general palette, but here everything has a livelier, folksier tone.

Details Define the Setting

Added light. To the left is the arched entrance leading to the back staircase. This hallway didn't receive much natural light, so I livened it up with a cheerful citrus yellow paint.

Cabinets and appliances. I furnished the kitchen with modern, stainless steel appliances to contrast with the mellow, Alder cabinets. The custom-made cabinets add much-needed storage in unusual places, like the narrow, floor-to-ceiling pull-out pantry (located to the right of the refrigerator) and the deeply recessed cabinet (above the refrigerator) for serving trays and extra dishes.

A working kitchen. The kitchen appliances are arranged in a classic triangular configuration. The center island—which houses the sink and dishwasher—serves as the primary workstation. The refrigerator and oven are within reach by simply turning around.

THE KITCHEN IN TRANSITION

The kitchen was one of the most challenging spaces in the house to redesign. It was evident that the kitchen had been updated repeatedly over the years. Attached to one side was a massive pantry that prevented the rear kitchen door from opening completely. As with almost every room in the house, the ceiling here had been dropped and the original plaster walls were covered with dark paneling. Fortunately, after the painstaking removal of several layers of old linoleum, I figured out the original configuration of the space by studying the scars left behind on the floor.

I decided to arch the new, open entryways to continue the Gothic theme in the architecture. I drew up a scaled plan for the space, which showed the placement of cabinets and appliances. After what seemed like months of planning and restructuring, I finalized the location of all base cabinets and appliances, mapping them out on the floor with masking tape. This allows you to get an idea of how much maneuverability your plan allows: Will your doors swing open all the way? Will you be able to lower the dishwasher and oven doors? Will you have to squeeze past the pantry to get to the stove? Imagine moving around in the space and make adjustments accordingly.

Before. (Top left and above) Here you can see the original kitchen, and how it looked after the room was gutted. Layers of old linoleum, paneling and dropped ceiling panels had to go before I was able to consider the arrangement of the basic kitchen units.

After. (Left) The new space bears almost no resemblance to what the kitchen looked like when I purchased the house. The floating center island makes room for additional, much needed workspace. The raised breakfast bar is perfect for entertaining. The space is comfortable, functional and beautiful.

A Scaled Rendering. A scaled rendering of the room is helpful for working out any kinks in the design beforehand. Occasionally, however, even the best-planned designs have to be modified as the work progresses. For example, once I began adding the textured stones around the perimeter of the arched openings (as depicted in the rendering), I felt the space was getting too busy, so I simplified the design and eliminated them.

The Heart of the Home. Hanging from the wrought iron pot rack are gleaming copper and stainless steel pots and pans—reinforcing the kitchen's lesson that the functional can also be beautiful. A colorful grouping of botanical prints anchor the back wall.

FAUX WOOD-GRAINED BEAMS

Nothing defines a classic country kitchen like the beauty of rough-hewn wood ceiling beams. Unfortunately, the prices for such architectural details can be exorbitant. As an inexpensive alternative, I built a frame to define the width and length of the beams, then covered it with plywood.

On top of this, I applied a faux-grained finish, complete with knots and texture; the result is instant rustic warmth. To create authenticity, I added "braces" to the beams. I hammered in long, "forged" nails, allowing some of the nail heads to protrude for effect.

During. The "beams" are constructed from inexpensive wood.

MATERIALS LIST

Joint compound; flexible putty knife; metal-toothed graining tool; 2-inch (51mm) chip brushes; detail artist brush; rags; paint tray; spray bottle; caulking gun; latex paintable interior caulk

Sherwin Williams Palette: 1. Black Bean 2. Harvest Gold 3. Aurora Brown 4. Bakelite Gold

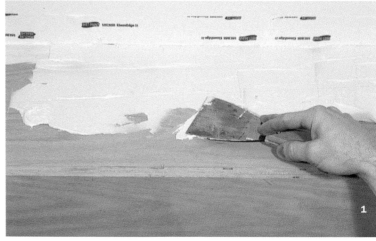

1 Coat beam with joint compound. Cover your floors and furniture with drop cloths before you begin. (Working with joint compound is messy.) Apply a liberal amount of joint compound to one side of the beam. Working on one side at a time allows you to create the graining pattern before the compound sets.

2 Create graining and ridges. Immediately after applying the joint compound, drag a metal graining or combing tool through the damp compound. Create a swirling, wavy horizontal path across the beam. Occasionally wipe the excess from the tool. Work as swiftly and loosely as possible. Don't be tempted to overwork the surface—swipe through it once and move on to the next section.

3 Create the knots. Let the beams dry overnight. Using a caulking gun loaded with latex paintable caulk, create knot outlines of various sizes, then swirl lines of caulking within each outline. Gently press the caulking into the background texture with a putty knife. You want the knot to be slightly raised but attached to the grained surface. (It helps to study real wood graining patterns.)

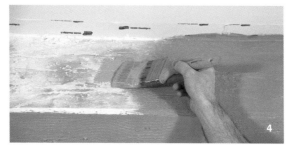

4 Basecoat the beams. Let the knots dry, prime the bare plaster, then apply a satin basecoat of a rich amber tone (I used Bakelite Gold) with a 2-inch (51mm) chip brush.

5 Paint the knots. Using an artist's brush, paint the center of each knot Aurora Brown, fading the color toward the outside. Lighten the raised areas around the knot by gently rubbing a damp rag across the surface. This should leave the dark color in the knot's crevices.

6 **Create the wood tone.** Paint each beam with several tones of browns, yellows or oranges, blending the colors to create an aged hue. To apply color, dip a 2-inch (51mm) chip brush in water, then pick up some color and scrub it over the surface. To make the colors mingle and blend, lightly mist the surface with water. Keep the color darker toward the edges, fading the color in the center. Softly drybrush the colors to blend.

"Iron" Braces. To enhance the rough-hewn, rustic feel of the beams, I added strips of pine wood, painted to look like iron braces. The tapered, "forged" nails complete the effect.

Before (Above).

CUSTOM WALL MURAL

Inspiration for murals can come from various sources. This mural was inspired by photos I took while traveling through Italy. The sun-faded, stuccoed, exterior walls of the homes that dotted the hillsides were the perfect inspiration. Time has a remarkable way of seasoning things. Capturing that worn appearance with paint was the challenge of this mural. Overall I wanted the kitchen to have a lived-in feel, comparable to a favorite pair of old jeans.

The wall space is limited, interrupted by windows, doors and cabinets. To make the walls appear unified, I laid a soft tone-on-tone color wash over the background, immediately giving the space more depth. It also suggests a relaxing mood. Over this, I painted the broken plaster walls with trompe l'oeil exposed brick and lath detailing. Before painting, I applied joint compound for texture, which adds a whimsical believability to the mural.

MATERIALS LIST

Joint compound; 1 ½-inch (37mm) and 3-inch (75mm) flexible putty knives; 2-inch (51mm) chip brushes; level; posterboard; chalk; pencil; tracing paper; graphite paper; rags; paint roller; disposable paint pans; artist's brushes; spray bottle; ¼-inch (6mm) automotive detailing tape

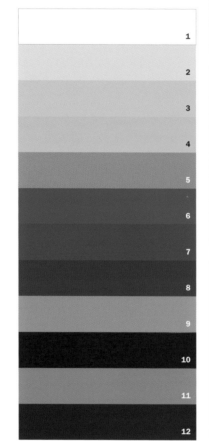

Sherwin Williams Palette: 1. Yellow Beam 2. Ambitious Amber 3. Viva Gold 4. Brittlebush 5. Caribbean Coral 6. Jay Blue 7. Rave Red 8. Roycroft Copper Red 9. Tupelo Tree 10. Roycroft Bottle Green 11. Knockout Orange 12. Turkish Coffee

1 Sketch the design. Over a neutral basecoat (here, Antique White), sketch an irregular outline of "breaks in the plaster" using chalk. Cut templates for the brick and lath shape from posterboard. Position the template, using a level if necessary, and trace around it with a pencil until all of the exposed laths and bricks are drawn.

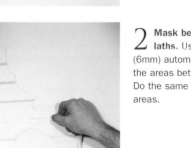

2 Mask between the laths. Using the ¼-inch (6mm) automotive tape, mask the areas between the laths. Do the same for the brick areas.

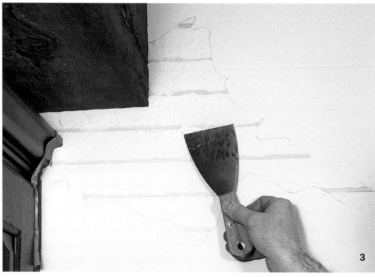

3 Apply joint compound to laths. Use 1 ½- (37mm) and 3-inch (75mm) flexible putty knives to sculpt the lath surfaces with joint compound. Leave a heavier bead at the edges, and feather out the compound toward the center of each board. Immediately remove the tape. Sculpt the outline of the "break in the plaster," using the same technique. Feather the compound into the smooth surrounding walls. Let the joint compound dry completely overnight. The next day, gently wipe the plastered areas with a damp rag to remove any rough or unnatural hard edges. Prime the bare joint compound with latex interior primer, then basecoat the area with Antique White.

4 **Apply joint compound to bricks.** Using the same techniques from the previous step, apply joint compound to the bricks.

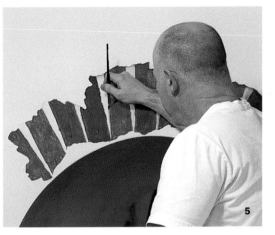

5 **Paint bricks.** Begin painting by filling in the bricks first. Don't paint all the bricks the same color. Load the brush with several tones at once and paint loosely. Scrub the color into the texture, mixing the multiple tones. Shadow and highlight the area, paying strict attention to the direction of any natural light source entering the room. Continue building the bricks until the desired depth of color is achieved.

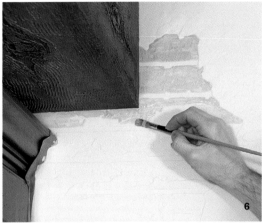

6 **Paint lath areas.** Paint the laths using the techniques in the previous step.

7 **Distress the laths.** Before the paint is completely dry, use a damp rag to lightly scrub off some of the paint from the center areas of the laths. This quick, effective technique adds the illusion of age and makes the painting more interesting. If you accidentally remove too much paint, simply layer on additional washes of color.

8 **Distress the bricks.** Distress the bricks using the techniques described in the previous step.

9 **Apply a color wash.** When the brick and lath details are completed, apply a tone-on-tone background color wash around the room. There are numerous ways to apply a latex wash, but I prefer to keep faux finishes simple, so I use an inexpensive, disposable 2-inch (51mm) chip brush, damp rags, a spray bottle filled with water, and two or three dollops of latex satin house paint. Begin at the top of the wall and work your way across and down, keeping the area ahead of you moist. Apply color slightly heavier around the corners and edges of the "exposed areas."

10 **Paint the ivy.** Freehand paint the ivy vines around the room. Load a liner brush with a dark green, and let the brush dance across the wall. Leave occasional breaks that you can later fill with ivy leaves. Highlight and shade the vine as you go, paying attention to the natural light source in the room. Using a square-edged brush and the base green color, sketch the ivy leaves as you go, varying their sizes and shapes.

11 **Detail the ivy.** After the initial layer dries, use a small liner brush to detail the individual leaves with veining. Add the vine's shadow to the wall using a dirty, black-brown mixture and a small liner brush.

12 **Add bugs and birds.** Add some whimsical details to your project by painting a few bugs, bees, birds or even a mouse. There's an abundance of available reference material for detail work like this. Simply enlarge the images to scale on tracing paper, then position them and transfer them to the wall with graphite paper. These simple additions really bring a mural to life!

The Mural View. (Above) The color transitions between rooms should blend naturally, especially in open passages. For the kitchen walls, a lighter, parchment-like version of the dining room finish was applied for uniformity. For whimsical detail, a pair of bees hover to the left of the arched opening. The terra cotta pig, artificial ivy and glazed bowl complete the rustic scene.

Behind the Counter. (Left) One of the great things about this type of loose-style mural is that only bits and pieces of the wall space will have to be hand-painted. The color wash background connects the areas, but the isolated areas of detail, like this area behind the island counter, go a long way to adding visual excitement to a room.

65

TROMPE L'OEIL TILED BACKSPLASH

Searching for the perfect size, color or pattern of tile can be an exhausting and costly venture. Making your own, on the other hand, is as visually and financially gratifying as it is fun! This project is a lot simpler than it may look. If you plan your tile layout and design carefully, and always check your measurements twice, the end result will truly "fool the eye!"

Inspired by Italy. The pattern on the hand-painted "tile" backsplash was adapted from Italian pottery. The bright, folksy colors are rustic and warm, yet have a certain sophistication.

MATERIALS LIST

Putty knife; ¼-inch (6mm) automotive detailing tape; measuring tape; straight-edge; pencil; round artist's brushes; 2-inch (51mm) chip brush; sandpaper (optional); polyurethane sealer (optional)

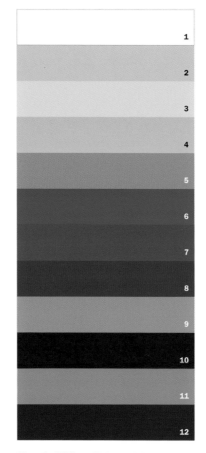

Sherwin Williams Palette: 1. Yellow Beam 2. Viva Gold 3. Ambitious Amber 4. Brittlebush 5. Caribbean Coral 6. Jay Blue 7. Rave Red 8. Copper Red 9. Tupelo Tree 10. Bottle Green 11. Knockout Orange 12. Turkish Coffee

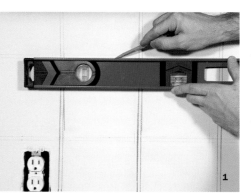

1 Create the tile design. Work out any kinks in tile placement or tile dimensions in advance by creating a scaled drawing. When figuring the layout on paper, be sure to include the ¼-inch (6mm) width of the grout areas, along with the dimensions of the tile. Lay out the tile design using a pencil and level for accuracy.

2 Mask grout areas. Mask the grout areas using ¼-inch (6mm) auto body detailing tape. Carefully align the tape, first horizontally, then vertically.

3 Form the tile. Form the tile using joint compound and flexible putty knives. Keep the outer edges thick—about a ¼-inch (6mm)—and feather out toward the center. You want to create a tumbled marble look, so irregular edges, skips and indentations in the joint compound are desirable. As soon as the tiles are formed, carefully remove the tape—first the vertical pieces, then the horizontal pieces.

When the joint compound has completely dried, vigorously rub a damp rag across each tile to soften any stiff ridges, peaks or edges. This will help to replicate the smooth feel of glazed, clay-fired tile.

4 **Paint the background.** Prime the bare joint compound with interior latex primer, then basecoat with Antique White. When this dries, apply a warm color wash by double-loading your brush with Yellow Beam and Viva Gold. Soften the brushstrokes before moving to the next tile by drybrushing. Don't try to match each tile. Paint swiftly and aim for an interesting variety in tones instead.

5 **Lift some paint.** Before the paint has completely dried—after painting three or four tiles—lightly rub the center of the tiles with a damp rag to give them a "halo" effect. After painting all the tiles, step back and make sure the color tones are balanced before proceeding.

6 **Draw the pattern.** Use a straightedge to draw the diagonal pattern on the tile. I painted the design freehand. If you're not comfortable freehanding, you can create a stencil instead and still get great results. The aim here is to duplicate the folk-art look of hand-painted Italian pottery. Each tile should be one of a kind!

7 **Define the diagonal yellow lines.** Use a brush that will hold a nice amount of paint (I used variously sized artist's brushes), and paint over the pencil outline.

8 **Paint the tiles.** Next, place the orange flower center followed by the red flower petals.

9 **Paint the tiles.** Follow next with the green leaf-like details, and then the blue flowers. Keep the brushstrokes simple and deliberate, and don't worry about slightly irregular edges. Liven up the decoration by accenting with a floating white highlight and a brown shading line, following the direction of any natural light entering the room. You can fool the eye even more by adding shadows under and to one side of each tile.

The tile can be left finished at this stage, or it can be distressed further by lightly sanding. Since this project will serve as a working backsplash, I applied three coats of high gloss sealer/polyurethane to prevent water and grease penetration.

FAUX-FRESCO RANGE HOOD

A decorative range hood is a charming architectural feature, often found in period kitchen settings. Though simply intended to hide the venting system above the range, a well-designed hood also serves as a centerpiece, perfect for hand-painted decoration. This work of art is the result of combining old architectural tin salvage, plastic grapes, joint compound and paint!

The center design. The center design was created by cutting a vintage tin panel (purchased at a local consignment shop) to fit within the inset, attaching it with construction adhesive. The sister panel is located above the mantel in the dining room (see page 43).

MATERIALS LIST

Joint compound; flexible putty knife; chalk; plastic grapes; scissors; glue gun and glue sticks; 2-inch (51mm) chip brushes; artist's brushes; paint pan; rags; water; 100-grit sandpaper; B-I-N or other suitable primer; polyurethane latex sealer (optional)

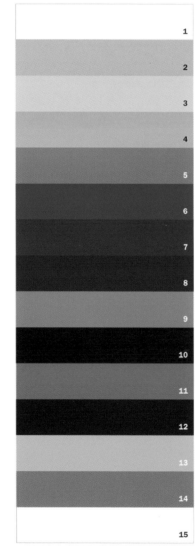

Sherwin Williams Palette: 1. Yellow Beam 2. Viva Gold 3. Ambitious Amber 4. Brittlebush 5. Caribbean Coral 6. Jay Blue 7. Rave Red 8. Copper Red 9. Tupelo Tree 10. Bottle Green 11. Knockout Orange 12. Turkish Coffee 13. Anjou Pear 14. Tatami Tan 15. Corona

The Range Hood's Construction. This hood was constructed using simple 2' × 4' (.6m × 1.2m) studs and drywall. To create the raised feel of the outer border, I cut a template of the desired shape using thick posterboard, and taped it into position onto the center of the hood. I next applied liberal amounts of joint compound around the perimeter of the template, slowly layering the joint compound until the desired depth of the border was achieved. The template was then carefully removed, revealing the arched inset, crowned by the fleur de lys detail.

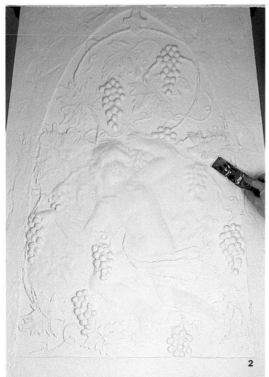

1 **Draw the design elements.** Using chalk, sketch the design elements on the hood: vines, leaves and grape bunches.

2 **Sculpt the leaves and vines.** Using joint compound and a putty knife, sculpt the additional leaves and stems. Build up a larger bead on the outside of the leaves and feather inward. Artist's palette knives work great for small details like this.

3 **Apply plastic grapes.** To create realistic grapes, take several bunches of artificial grapes, wash them to remove any oil or residue, then cut them in half. Using a hot glue gun, attach the grape halves to the hood in clusters according to the design. Add swirls and twig details with a caulk gun and paintable latex caulking. Seal the surface with a coat of B-I-N primer which will prepare the plastic surface for painting.

4 **Unify the design elements.** Brush a thinned coat of joint compound over the entire inset to unify the new elements with the rest of the piece. The joint compound falls into the crevices of the grapes and around the caulked elements, unifying the surfaces for a smoother paint surface.

5 **Basecoat and mottle the background.** When the joint compound is completely dry, apply a multicolored wash over the entire hood using Anjou Pear, Tatami Tan and Corona. Pour a dollop of each color into the corners of a disposable paint pan. Mist a working area with water, then double load a 2-inch (51mm) chip brush, picking up a tiny amount of each paint. Randomly scrub the paint into the misted area. Use a damp rag to mottle and spread the tone, blending the various colors into one another. Lightly drybrush the area to eliminate any marks left by the brush or rag.

6 **Paint the scene.** Paint the details of the design using a combination of round and square-tipped artist's brushes. Paint the leaves and stems first, then the grapes, and finally the flesh-toned cherub. Use the basic shading and highlighting techniques as you apply the details, and watch the hood come to life!

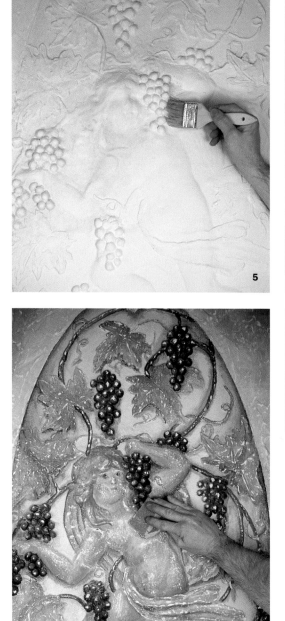

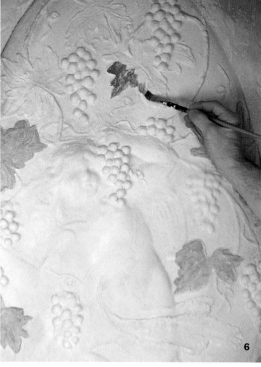

7 **Distress the surface.** Using 100-grit sandpaper, gently distress the completed painted hood by sanding the raised areas. To soften any abrasive mars left by the sand paper, apply a thinned wash of "dirty" color using a 2-inch (51mm) chip brush. Focus on the raised areas. The resulting finish should resemble a delicate, worn fresco.

TIME ON YOUR SIDE

Decorative art takes time to be fully realized. Faux finishes often require layering processes, and murals are often detail-oriented. The decorative artist's best resource is time.

Lighting is Key. Lighting plays an important part in planning a kitchen. Combine new and old fixtures to create wonderful ambient- and task-lighting solutions. The pair of Gothic hanging pendant chandeliers serve as the main lighting for the room. Large recess lighting over the island provides sufficient working light, while smaller, accent recess lighting highlights the cupboards and artwork.

Undercounter pocket lights blanket the countertops with a warm glow, and interior perimeter lighting accents the leaded-glass windows and colorful glassware inside the wall cabinets.

LAYERED TEXTURES

The rustic atmosphere in the kitchen is created by the various textures: hammered copper farmhouse sink; rippled stained-glass; knotty alder cabinets; rubbed pewter hardware; distressed bead board; delicately threaded, sheer window treatments; sleek, stainless steel appliances; porous-looking, multicolored quartz countertops; textured and muraled walls; stone and tumbled-marble flooring; heavily grained and textured faux-wooden beams. The surfaces evoke an old-fashioned charm, as the natural-looking patinas give the kitchen a "well-lived" feeling.

Whimsical details are an important part of every home, like the bugs and birds that have taken up residence throughout mine. Unexpected whimsy often reflects the homeowner's personality and interests; it breaks the sterile feel of serious décor by adding a jolt of unexpected color and humor.

A Warm Wood. The rich color of the alder wood instantly warms the room. The finish is a mellow, pecan-colored glaze, gently distressed with hand-rubbed ebony highlights peeking out. Large, exposed knots and split-grain accents in the wood add an aged, comfortable texture to the room.

A Sweet Touch. An old-fashioned cupboard anchors the rear wall, complete with bead board backing and custom leaded-glass inserts. The Gothic panels are sweetened by the addition of whimsical, three-dimensional butterflies, an ant and a caterpillar.

Details like the dappled textured green bowl of apples, hand-colored botanical prints, and simple, richly colored dish towel, are easy solutions for incorporating the house's rich accent palette.

CaesarStone. The island's raised bar area is perfect for breakfast or for guests to mingle behind as dinner is prepared. The countertops are made from CaesarStone, an extremely durable, man-made quartz composite surface, comparable to granite.

Hardware. The twisted roping of the distressed pewter handles echoes the original spindle design in the foyer staircase. Likewise, the floret pattern stamped on the knob reflects the floral motif.

A Working Kitchen. The island features a fabulous copper farmhouse sink. Its hand-hammered finish glows against the dark-grained cabinet. The vintage-style copper faucet adds period grace to the scene. The dishwasher is located to the left of the sink. To the sink's right is a handy pull-out spice rack and waste receptacle cabinet.

STUDY & OFFICE

THE SECOND-FLOOR STUDY (formerly the master bedroom) is actually two rooms. One room serves as a home office, complete with built-in file drawers flanking an antique, gilded desk. The other room, the study, is home to a wall-to-wall, custom-built bookcase and entertainment unit, reading and lounging areas, and a faux wood-grained fireplace. My intent was to make these areas rich in color and texture.

Faux finishing can quickly dominate a room, so one of my favorite decorating techniques is to single out one wall or the ceiling of a room for a "wow" element. As an accent to a basic wall color, the faux finishing is more aesthetically pleasing. The study and office have gone beyond that. I pushed the number of visual elements here. What keeps it from overwhelming the eye is the fact that everything is subtly related. Each finish is dramatic—the richly toned faux leather, the crackled built-ins, the dimensional ceiling mural, the wood-grained mantel and the faux-limestone blocks—yet the color palettes support each other. The earthy brown tones in each finish link the colors, so that no one finish steals the show.

Though the handsome room exudes a masculine feel, it still has a warm, cozy essence that invites you in.

After Construction. (Above) Originally, I prepped the walls with a deep teal, but the color seemed too dark and moody. I replaced it with a rich "tomato soup" color. It's the perfect base tone for the warm, faux-leather finish.

The Finished Study. (At right) The room is appointed with an eclectic mix of new and old furnishings, including new, soft leather recliners paired with a hand-embroidered, antique armchair. An oversized faux-tortoise shell coffee table fronts a deep, loose-pillowed luxury sofa.

Details Define the Setting

Contrasting color. Though I decided not to paint the room with the dark teal tone, I kept many of the teal accents in the window treatments, as well as in my prized collections of Italian gilded boxes, crackle glass and artist figurines. It proves just how effective opposite colors (in this case, red and blue-green) can be.

Vibrant flavor. The vibrant oil paintings above the mantel and in the office are the work of Quebec artist Raynald Leclerc. Though the scenes are Canadian, they remind me of the Ohio River valley; the steeples in these paintings are very reminiscent of the churches in my neighborhood.

Architectural décor. The inlaid hardwood floor medallion—painstakingly crafted on-site—centers the room. The craftspeople used various exotic woods to compose the design, surrounding it with a field of red oak and a Brazilian rosewood border.

FAUX-LEATHER WALLS

One of my favorite wall finishes is faux leather. Clients also seem to love the seductive look and exotic texture of this finish. What makes it unique is that the walls are painted to look as if actual panels of leather have been stitched together. This is an easy finish to execute, making it the perfect project for busy homeowners.

The secret to a successful faux leather finish lies in the combination of colors, which should be deep and richly saturated. My favorites are shades of red, brown, orange and ochre, though any deep-valued tone can be used. If you're unsure about the colors, take the extra time to experiment with a sample board, or hire a color expert or interior designer for advice.

The leather look is traditionally used in the study or home office, but it works well in any room of the house.

SECTIONING THE WALL

Although you don't have to section off the wall with tape, you'll find that the finish is more manageable if you do. With individual panels taped off, there's less worry about keeping a wet edge, and you can take a break between panels.

MATERIALS LIST

Measuring tape; blue painter's tape; 2-inch (51mm) chip brushes; spray bottle; 5 yards (4.5m) polished cotton for rag rolling; black fine-tip permanent marker; oil-glazing liquid; mineral spirits; empty 1-gallon (4-liter) container; sponge roller; paint pan; rubber gloves

Sherwin Williams Palette: 1. Determined Orange **2.** Sturdy Brown **3.** Aurora Brown **4.** Roycraft Copper Red **5.** Sable

1 Basecoat the walls. Basecoat the walls with satin latex paint (Determined Orange). After the paint dries, measure the walls and divide the space into equal panels. Tape off every other panel. The aim is to shade the individual panels with a dirty "halo" effect. To do this, double load the 2-inch (51mm) chip brush with Roycraft Copper Red and Sturdy Brown, and apply the paint. Dip the brush in water occasionally to keep the paints diluted enough to move fluidly. Keep the application heaviest around the seam lines. Fade it towards the center of each panel by pouncing lightly. You can also use a damp rag to fade the color toward the center. When the first panels are shaded, remove and reposition the tape to complete the adjacent panels.

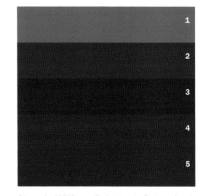

2 Draw the stitch seam. Remove the tape to reveal the seams in the leather panels. For additional interest, add a trompe l'oeil stitch to the seam by following the seam with a black, fine-tip permanent marker and leaving irregular skips or jolts. Go back to the top and add alternating arched "stitches."

3 Glaze the panels. Mix a glaze of 2 parts oil glazing liquid and 1 part mineral spirits. Slowly add oil-based tint (here, semigloss Sturdy Brown and Aurora Brown). The mixture should be either darker or lighter than the underlying base tones, depending on the look you want. I prefer to apply a darker glaze in a tone similar to my basecoat, yet contrasting enough that the glow of the base color will bleed through. The glaze should have the consistency of thick motor oil.

Roll the glaze onto an individual panel, using a 12-inch (30cm) sponge roller. Remember a little glaze will go a long way, so remove most of the glaze from the roller prior to applying. Lay an even, but fairly thick coat onto the panel. Immediately proceed with the next step before applying glaze to adjacent panels.

4

4 **Ragroll the walls.** To ragroll, use slightly stiff, polished cotton fabric cut into pieces about 2' × 4' (51mm × 10cm). Prepare the pieces in advance, making sure you have enough on hand to ragroll the entire room. One piece can be used on 2 to 4 panels, depending on the length of the panels and how crisp you want the texture to be.

While the glaze is still wet, crumble a cloth accordian-fashion, then twist it. Holding the fabric loosely, start at the ceiling edge and gently "walk" the rag down the wall, picking up glaze as you go. Crumble the cloth occasionally to keep the amount of glaze removed as even as possible. (The more saturated the rag, the less glaze it will pick up.) To avoid noticeable stops and starts, try to keep the breaks uneven. Continue glazing and ragrolling the adjacent panels.

PRETTY BUT STUBBORN

I recommend wearing rubber gloves when working with oil glaze. It can be difficult to remove from your hands later on.

A Well-Appointed Library. (Right) The inlaid floor medallion is a focal point in this stately room. Warm, glossy hardwoods accentuate the faux leather walls and ceiling mural.

Manipulate the Architecture:

FAUX LIMESTONE WALL

Sometimes I'm confronted with the challenge of pulling together adjacent areas (e.g., here in the office and study) that share a common wall or open passageway, but have no trim molding or doors to define them. A great solution, I've discovered, is to use the thickness of the wall to suggest large slabs or blocks of stone, such as marble or brick.

I applied this finish to the elaborate ceiling soffit framing the figurative mural, as well as to the fireplace, creating the illusion that it was architecturally supporting the soffit above. With a little paint and creativity, you can manipulate the architecture of a space, transforming a room without using a single nail or hammer!

MATERIALS LIST

1-inch (25mm) blue painter's tape; tape measure; 2-inch (51mm) chip brushes; latex or acrylic paints (brown, black and tan tones); terry cloth rags; Faux Effects Set-Coat/Clear, Faux Effects FauxCreme/Clear latex glazing liquid; Faux Effects FauxCreme Colors tints (Earth Brown, Van Dyke Brown, Chestnut Brown); posterboard; Faux Effects Activator II; protective eyeware; wide foam brush; mixing containers; small, round artist's brush; whiz rollers

Sherwin Williams Palette: 1. Restrained Gold 2. Tatami Tan 3. Black of Night 4. Aurora Brown.

1 **Basecoat and shade the blocks.** Basecoat with warm beige in a satin finish. Measure the stone pattern, then take 1-inch (25mm) blue painter's tape, tear both sides to create ragged edges, and lay it down to form the irregularly shaped grout lines.

Shade each block individually by simultaneously applying three latex tones—brown, black and tan. Using a 2-inch (51mm) brush, apply the tone heaviest around the perimeter, softening it toward the center. Occasionally spray the block with water to help move the paint around.

2 **Mottle the color and apply sealer.** Mottle the colors while they are still wet using a damp rag. Leave the center rather soft with the edges more defined and "dirty." When dry, apply a liberal coat of Setcoat with a whiz roller. This clear sealant will prepare the walls for further distressing. Let dry overnight.

3 **Apply color glazes.** Using FauxCreme/Clear latex glazing, prepare three batches of color in separate containers. Tint with three tones of FauxCreme Color: Earth Brown, Van Dyke Brown and Chestnut Brown. Swirl the tones randomly on each block using a 2-inch (51cm) chip brush.

4 **Blend the tones.** Pounce the glazes immediately with a damp rag, using the cloth to blend the tones. To create realistic ridges in the limestone, place a torn piece of posterboard in the still-wet glaze. Pounce the rag toward the ragged edge of the posterboard, then lift the board away. A crisp line will form in the glaze, similar to the natural ridges found in quarried limestone.

5 **Apply activator.** Before the glaze sets, use Faux Effects Activator no. 2 to create pits and variations in the limestone. Pour a small amount of the activator into a pail, dip your fingers into it, and flick the activator onto the glazed surface. (Don't apply too much or undesirable runs may form.) The activator sets in about 15 minutes, so work in manageable portions. Wear protective glasses and gloves, and protect adjacent areas and floors with drop cloths.

6 **Lift activator and distress surface.** Let the activator work for approximately 15 minutes, then pounce the surface with a dry rag to lift color and reveal the pits and variations. This is a very physical step, requiring patience and muscle, but the results are realistic pits and valleys that are well worth the effort. To further emphasize the appearance of limestone, gently drag a wide foam brush across the surface of each block in random directions.

7 **Paint the grout shadows.** Remove the blue painter's tape and paint the grout areas using black and brown. Following the direction of any natural light in the room, add a dark shadow under each block and to the appropriate side of it. Add a final sealant if desired.

The handsome wool drapery acts as a sound barrier for the entertainment center's surround-sound acoustics and protects the room from extreme temperature variations.

Most of the artwork in the room depicts religious icons or churches, like this hand-colored etching of Notre Dame Cathedral in Paris.

A hammered-copper table is paired with a faux-bronzed iron lamp with a blue parchment shade; the contrast of the warm and cool colors, as well as the differences in the textures, encapsulate the room's palette.

Distinct but Unified. To keep the study and the office notably separate, I painted the wall with a faux limestone finish, complete with "fossil" details. To unify the spaces, a leopard-like crackle finish was applied to the floor-to-ceiling bookcases in each area. The red faux leather and the custom-made teal wool window dressings balance the color in each room.

Embellish It:

FAUX WOOD-GRAINED MANTEL

The new mantel arrived from the Mission Stone factory (see page 32 for resource information) with a faux-limestone finish, which didn't work with what I had in mind. Instead, I transformed it into this dark, dramatic, carved-wood masterpiece. It's hard to believe, but this is the same mantel that's in the parlor. The added rubber embellishments from Pearlworks—the "carved" griffins with the acanthus scrollwork and the decorative mantel brackets—totally altered the feel of the fireplace. The rich Burnt Sienna finish has a warm, mellow patina. The finish was simple to execute and adds considerable sophistication and beauty to the room.

RESOURCES

Pearlworks, Inc.
14251 Franklin Avenue
Tustin CA 92780
Phone: 1-888-25-PEARL (73275)
Website: www.pearlworksinc.com

MATERIALS LIST

mineral spirits; 2-inch (51mm) chip brushes; black latex satin paint; rags; water; Minwax wood finish in Provincial no. 211

Sherwin Williams Palette: 1. Butterfield 2. French Roast 3. Black Bean

Embellishments. These flexible rubber embellishments, obtained from Pearlworks Architectural Details, were applied to the mantle using a liquid adhesive.

1 **Basecoat the mantel.** Paint the mantel a mustard brown using an oil semigloss finish. The oil semigloss will adhere to the surface well and withstand the heat from a working fireplace.

2 **Antique the carving.** Using Black Bean and French Roast, paint wet-on-wet to "age" the mantel's carvings and edges. Using a 2-inch (51mm) chip brush, push the colors into the crevices. Immediately wipe color from the raised areas with a damp rag.

3 **Drybrush and seal.** Lightly drybrush the brown and black latex tones from step 2 around the lines of the mantel to build up a convincing sooty, aged feel.
Brush the entire mantel with Minwax wood finish. This gives it a realistic wood-toned appearance, while providing a durable protective coat.

The Mantel Before and After. The home's Gothic theme is furthered by the addition of the winged griffins holding a shield and the acanthus scrollwork and brackets. The brick-patterned surround was cut from ceramic tile. The original cast iron decoration of the firebox was cleaned, then drybrushed with gold metallic paint to accent its beautiful detail. The stamped concrete hearth blends seamlessly with the tiled surround and is accented with a band of Brazilian rosewood. Collectively, the limestone, leather and wood-grained paint finishes have a timeworn feel that's fitting for this comfortable setting.

CRACKLE-FINISH BOOKCASES

Installing custom-built cabinets and bookcases can add significant value and beauty to a home. This is particularly true in older homes, such as this one, which tend to have little or no storage space. I decided to design floor-to-ceiling wall units for both the office and study areas. The study's main unit provides housing for all my media equipment, as well as storage space for CD and video collections, which are hidden behind the raised panel doors. The office unit is designed around the carved desk that I found at a local antique shop. Nestled between handy file drawers, the desk's delicately carved and gilded legs appear right at home.

I decided to create an exotic, leopard-skin crackle finish for the units. The sheer number of drawers, panels and shelves made this a time-consuming task, but the results are dazzling. The vibrant gold undercoat gleams beneath the coffee-colored top coat, creating architectural interest in the spaces. For extra pizazz, I emphasized the fluted columns and decorative capitals with gold leaf.

Wall Sconce.
I found this pair of wrought-iron and pressed-tin sconces at a local flea market. I love the looped arms and acanthus details. I left the rustic finish as is, but for safety's sake, I updated the wiring.

MATERIALS LIST

Faux Effects SetCoat/Clear; Faux Effects AquaSize; Faux Effects AquaCrackle/Clear; Faux Effects FauxCreme color tints (Van Dyke Brown, Dark Brown, Burnt Sienna, Rouge Royale); Imitation Dutch Metal gold leaf; Wunda Size sizing; softening brush; no. 3 steel wool; 2-inch (51mm) chip brushes; whiz rollers.

Sherwin Williams Palette: 1. French Roast 2. Butterfield

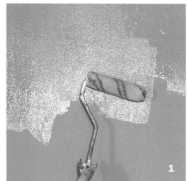

1 **Basecoat and seal the wood.** Basecoat the units with two coats of a buttery yellow in a satin latex finish. When this is dry, apply a coat of Faux Effects Setcoat (Clear) using a chip brush and whiz type roller. This product seals the surface and prepares it for the crackling process. Let dry thoroughly overnight before proceeding.

2 **Apply sizing.** Using a 2-inch (51mm) chip brush, apply by brush and/or roller a liberal coat of Faux Effects AquaSize. This milky, colorless material will set in approximately 30 minutes. Be ready to immediately apply the crackle medium when the sizing turns from milk to clear.

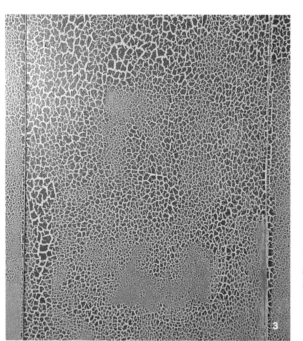

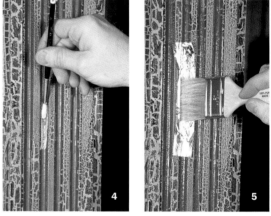

3 **Apply crackle medium.** When the sizing no longer appears milky, the surface is ready for the crackle top coat application. Tint the colorless AquaCrackle with FauxCreme Color tints (I mixed Van Dyke Brown and Dark Brown with one batch of AquaCrackle, and Burnt Sienna, Dark Brown and Rouge Royale with the other). Randomly apply swirls of the lighter, reddish tone (see photo step 2). Using a whiz roller, blend the dark brown tone into it. In approximately 15 minutes, cracks will begin forming. Let dry overnight.

4 **Apply sizing.** Using a warm, deep-red tone, basecoat the areas you plan to gild. (This will really make the gold leaf glisten.) Let dry, then apply the sizing where you'll be laying gold leaf. When the sizing dries to a clear sheen (in about 15 minutes), it's ready for gilding.

5 **Apply gold leaf.** Press the gold leaf sheets onto the sized areas and brush off the excess with a soft brush. I chose to further distress and soften the glow by gently sanding with coarse no. 3 steel wool. Seal the entire surface to protect the gold leaf from tarnishing.

A Stately Effect. The wall of custom cabinetry and bookshelves has a stately presence in the library. The contrasting leopard-like crackle finish gives the room an exotic ambiance. The antique throne chair with its floral needlepoint pairs comfortably with the back-drop. Family mementos and knick-knack collections soften the masculine tone.

MONOCHROMATIC FIGURATIVE MURAL

The tray ceiling in the study was specially constructed to show-case a mural. I chose to paint a Michelangelo-esque figurative representation in a simple monochromatic palette.

The process of layering a single color in multiple shades can result in more dimensionality than you might expect. This style of painting is formally referred to as "grisaille," from the French word "gris" for gray, because shades of black and white were often used.

I decided to use a Burnt Sienna palette to balance out the darker tones of the room. For additional drama, I layered the mural with a nicotine-hued, crackled patina to suggest age. The softly mottled amber hues infuse the room with warmth.

MATERIALS LIST

Assorted square-tipped artist's brushes; rags; paint tray and disposable liners; small container of water; 2-inch (51mm) chip brushes; Faux Effects Setcoat/clear; Faux Effects Aqua Finishing Solutions AquaSize/clear; Faux Effects AquaCrackle/clear; Faux Effects FauxCreme; Faux Effects FauxCreme Color Tints in Yellow Ochre and Van Dyke Brown; 4-inch (10cm) round pouncing brush; spray bottle

Sherwin Williams Palette: 1. Leather Bound

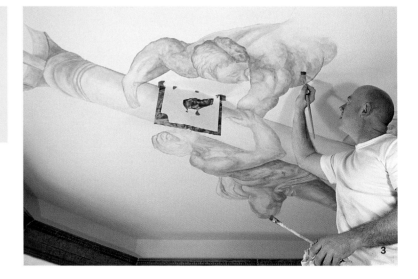

1 **Start with the design.** Design the mural and transfer your composition to the ceiling.

2 **Sketch the outlines.** Load a square-tipped artist brush with a dab of Leather Band satin latex paint. With a wet rag in hand to move and lift paint, sketch the figures' outlines.

3 **Layer the color.** To build up the muscle shapes, continue to layer the color until the desired depth is achieved. Latex paint dries very quickly, so apply additional washes of color immediately. Figure painting, especially on a ceiling, can be intimidating. I find it helpful to concentrate on one area at a time, like an arm or stomach muscle, instead of the whole body. The mural will quickly begin to take shape.

REFER FOR ACCURACY

Always refer back to your reference material for accuracy. It's helpful to "isolate" the individual figure you're working on in the reference drawing with white paper.

4 **Fine-tune the detail.** Continue painting until you've attained a balanced color throughout the mural. Create, soft atmospheric clouds by swirling a 2-inch (51mm) chip brush, loaded with lightened color, around the background. Use a damp rag to swirl the paint around. Spritz the areas you're working on occasionally to maintain a wet edge and produce an airy, atmospheric background. I painted an occasional cloud over the scene, which pushes the figures back and adds an amazing sense of dimension.

5 **Prepare the surface for the crackle finish.** Prepare the mural for a crackling by coating it with FauxEffects Setcoat/clear. Apply a generous coat with a roller, and let it dry overnight. Next, apply a coat of clear AquaSize. To create larger cracks here and there, apply it more heavily in certain areas. When the milky color of the AquaSize clears, the surface is ready for the crackle medium.

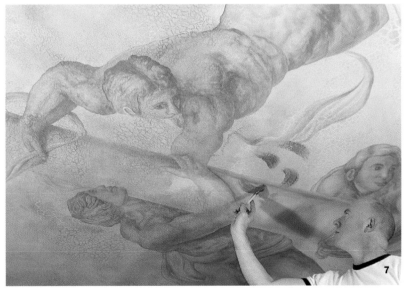

6 **Apply crackle medium.** Tint the clear AquaCrackle slightly with a yellow ochre FauxCreme Color Tint. This gives the crackling an old, varnished look when dry. When tinting the crackle medium, remember that the color will dry several shades darker than it appears when mixed. For best results, test on a piece of scrap posterboard (dry it with a hair dryer if you're in a hurry) before rolling it onto the ceiling. For deeply crusted results, apply the crackle medium heavily with the roller. Cracks will begin forming within 15 minutes of application. Let dry overnight.

7 **Apply antiquing glaze.** Tint the FauxCreme with FauxCreme Color Tint in Van Dyke Brown. Apply the glaze in random swirls with a 2-inch (51mm) chip brush.

8 **Burnish the color in.** Force the color into the cracks by rubbing vigorously with a rounded 4-inch (10cm) pouncing brush. (This specialty brush is often used to apply the swirling texture patterns on stamped ceilings and can usually be found in local hardware stores.)

9 **Remove excess glaze.** To remove excess glaze, lightly dab a crumpled rag or foam brush across the surface in random directions. When dry, the ceiling can be sealed with either a clear or tinted glaze or with polyurethane.

AVOID A SORE NECK

Whenever you step down to check your work (which you should do frequently), take the opportunity to look around the room and roll your head gently to loosen your neck muscles. Keeping your head tilted back with no break will give you a very sore neck.

The Construction. (Top) The soffit was originally built to accommodate the new central-heating and air-conditioning system.

The Effect. (Above) I framed the mural with detailed crown molding. The rope lighting, tucked along the perimeter of the molding, floods the ceiling with an inviting glow.

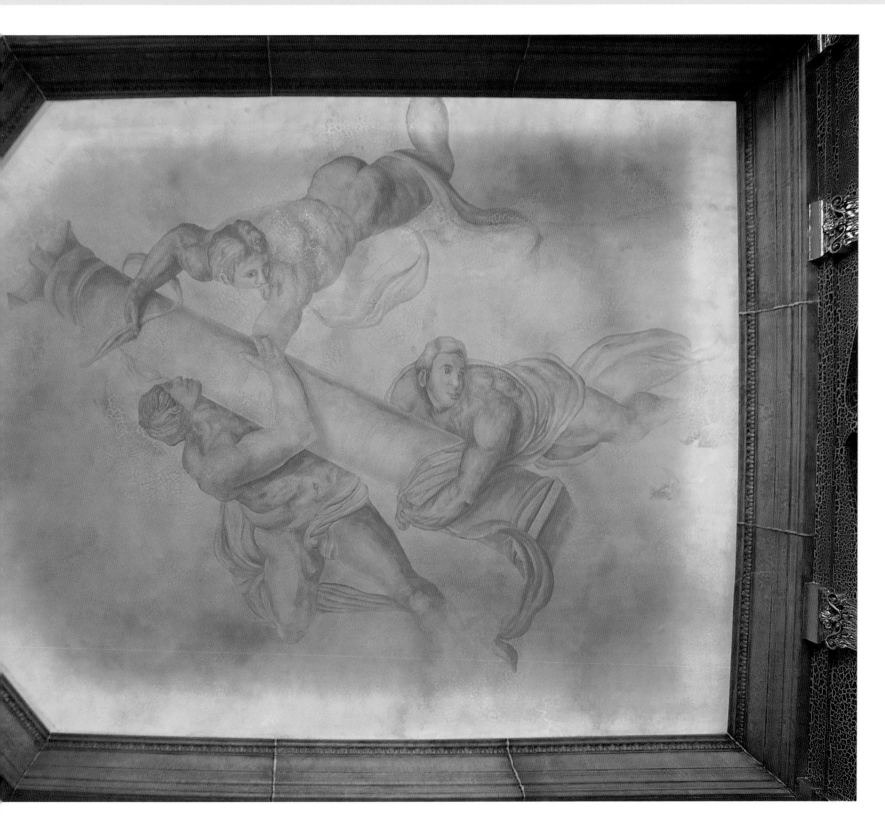

FAUX-BRONZED CEILING MEDALLION

I found this blown-glass chandelier, which hangs prominently in my home office, at a home improvement store. Its dainty, wrought-iron scrolls secure the colorful glass bowl, casting a warm glow on the faux-bronzed plaster medallion above. The color of the bowl itself is quite bright and saturated. It works surprisingly well in the soberly hued study. This just goes to show that you should experiment with the colors in your palette when you accessorize.

I purchased the Gothic-style ceiling medallion from Boston Ornament Company, which specializes in historical reproduction embellishments.

MATERIALS LIST

2-inch (51mm) chip brush; square-tipped artist brush; Modern Masters Metallic Paint in Antique Bronze; gold metallic acrylic paint

Sherwin Williams Palette: 1. French Roast

RESOURCES

Boston Ornament Company
20 Fordham Street
Allston, MA 02134
Phone: (617) 787-4118
Website: www.bostonornament.com

1 **Paint the medallion.** Basecoat the plaster medallion with a dark, rich brown in a satin finish. Let dry, then drybrush the entire piece with a metallic bronze-toned latex paint using a 2-inch (51mm) chip brush.

2 **Add accent color.** As a final accent, use a small artist's brush to drybrush some of the raised decoration with gold metallic latex paint. The end result is a simple, yet convincing, flourish.

Glowing Warmth. This modern piece of art glass has such an odd mix of colors—the saturated olive and red accent tones float in a sea of rich mustard—that I can't help but love it.

A Little Color. These brightly colored miniature jugs and vases bring cheer to my bookshelves. When I have a dinner party, I fill them with tiny bouquets and set them around the table.

I've always been drawn to rich color, especially in vibrant, sparkling glassware. Over the years, I've scoured yard sales and country auctions for multicolored vintage crackle glass. The fine texture of its cracked veining delights me.

As a young child, I was fascinated by my Aunt Lottie's old, translucent amber vase. It sat near her living room picture window and, when the sun streamed through the wavy and pitted windowpane, reflected the light to form a spectacular golden starburst on the opposite wall.

Because of its ability to capture and transform light, I tend to decorate with glass often, showcasing it under recessed lighting and using it to bring life to dark areas.

This three-color latex wash goes a long way to warming up the narrow, second-floor hall. The citrus shades of apricot, blush and melon were inspired by the warm tones in the hand-blown glass chandelier hanging in the background office.

Color washing with latex house paint, while simple and effective, is physically tiring. The color has to be scrubbed onto the walls and rapidly feathered out before the quick-drying latex paint sets. The idea behind this finish is to create irregularly patterned, diamond-shaped blotches on the wall. These shapes merge and overlap, adding a deeper dimension to the space. The three colors can be applied in any order, but I recommend applying a single color at a time. Layering single washes results in an infinite rainbow of tone-on-tone color. The more layers you add, the more depth you'll achieve, making this finish perfect for creating the illusion of space in any small corridor or room.

MATERIALS LIST

2-inch (51mm) chip brush; water; rags; spray bottle; paint tray

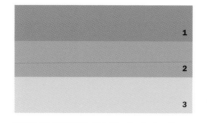

Sherwin Williams Palette: 1. Emberglow 2. Ravishing Coral 3. Avid Apricot

1 **Apply paint.** Spray a 4' × 4' (1.2m × 1.2m) working area with water. Dip a damp, 2-inch (51mm) chip brush randomly into multiple colors, picking up small amounts of color at a time. Apply the paint in an irregular diamond format, mottling the colors as you go.

2 **Soften the color.** While the paint is still wet, blend and feather out the colors with a damp rag, leaving the color lighter in the middle of the diamond shape. The result creates a subtle, tone-on-tone, atmospheric finish.

The Hallway as Gallery. The narrow hall leads to the rear laundry room and up to the third-floor master suite. It serves as a gallery area, showcasing a favorite trio of exotic botanical prints I found while on holiday in Hawaii. When traveling, I always try to purchase local artwork. It's a wonderful memento; but just as importantly, it supports the local arts community.

Gallery Hall Looking Toward Office. The dark passageway is brightened by the atmospheric color wash. I purchased the vintage, 1950s painted cupboard at a yard sale. I love how the arched panel looks like a niche with a vase of flowers.

I encourage clients to display their family history, personal accomplishments and general interests in their homes. The objects that define who we are—like precious mementos, family photographs, athletic and artistic awards, scholastic and professional achievements—should also define the space we live in. Why leave these treasures to collect dust in lidded boxes or unopened storage closets? Celebrate your accomplishments and passions!

The collections in my home are abundant and varied. Some are simple and utilitarian, like the arrangement of wooden picture frames that serves to conceal a vent. Other collections exist strictly for beauty and color, like the decorative glazed dishes and platters along the dining room plate ledge. Some are personal, like the treasured miniature artist's easels and porcelain figurines—many of which were gifts from clients and friends. Still others reflect a historical note, like the childhood county fair and scholastic ribbons casually draped on a shelf in the library, or the neatly grouped watercolor renderings in the studio (representing a sample of murals I've been commissioned to do over the past 20 years).

Whatever the subject, collections feed your soul and educate others about who you are and what inspires you. Happy collecting!

1. Displays of Something Different. Instead of the traditional mirror above the parlor mantel, there is a group of gilded, wooden sconces from Italy. Boldly paired with them is a growing collection of vintage English lusterware. **2. Display of Practicality.** These watercolor sketches of my murals conceal an awkward vent in the upstairs studio area. **3. Display to Balance.** I love to hang art or mirrors over mural paintings. They soften the preciousness of exotic, hand-painted finishes. **4. Displays of Affection and Humor.** The shelves in the study make great display cases. The miniature easels (left on facing page) and the figurines and decorative boxes (right on facing page) were gifts from friends and clients. The award ribbons (left on this page) add a touch of color and nostalgia. The dog photos and figurines (right on this page) guard the books about canine behavior.

GUESTROOM

G UESTROOMS should be designed with the guests' pleasure in mind, providing maximum comfort and luxury. This guestroom's comfort level and luxuriousness blend well: the full-room mural, custom window- and bed-dressings, wall-to-wall carpeting, fireplace and antique furnishings, all serve to elegantly pamper overnight guests.

Infusing guestrooms with color is vital; most visitors are bored with white or neutral bedrooms. Color dominates this room; and the full-room, chinoiserie mural sets the tone. The vibrant Chinese garden landscape is intricately rendered on what appears to be fine, silk canvas. A mural like this one inspires guests' imaginations, adding an exotic ambiance to the overnight experience.

When you enter a space with a full-room mural, you become part of the story and are transported to the world it depicts; this is exactly the

Guestroom Before. (Top) The dark paneling and dropped ceilings did very little to make this room inviting. **Guestroom During Demolition.** (Above) The basic bones of the room were good, as you can see with the paneling and carpeting removed.

effect a well-designed, well-executed mural should have on the viewer. It is a lucky guest that rests in this bedroom, enveloped by its tranquil beauty and irresistible charm.

Timeless Quality. (Right) A modern, beaded- and tufted-silk fabric adds significant texture and drama to the room. Draped at the footboard is a Victorian crazy quilt, composed of richly muted velvet scraps. The contrasting textures of the fabrics and exaggerated stitching and embellishments balance each other.

Details Define the Setting

Antique cast-iron bed. This treasured bed was one of my first major investments in antiques. I love its original finish and exposed layers of paint and rust. To preserve the wonderful patina, I coat the iron with rubbed linseed oil once a year. This gives the surface a beautiful, low-luster sheen to the surface.

French-style commodes. Flanking the bed are a pair of miniature bird's-eye maple commodes. The golden color and pitted graining contrast nicely with the soft mural, while the dark green marble tops harmonize with the hilly foreground.

Embroidered silk fabric. The shimmering celadon silk of the window treatment is intensified with embroidered flowering vines. I discovered the fabric after painting the wall mural, even though it appears to have suggested the theme.

Print collection. This is one of my favorite collections, assembled over many years. There are two scenes portrayed in the prints, both depicting mythological merriment. Most are in their original gilded- or black-lacquered frames. The height of the collection balances the towering fireplace opposite the bed.

CHINOISERIE-INSPIRED GARDEN MURAL

There are several factors to consider before attempting a full-room mural. Foremost is the architectural workability of the room itself (i.e., whether the space is conducive to mural work). Is there adequate lighting, both natural and incandescent, to properly illuminate a floor-to-ceiling mural? Is there ample room to appreciate the mural from a distance? Is there at least one good vantage point from which the viewer will be able to take in the mural and perceive a thematic connection from corner to corner? Is the subject matter appropriate to the style of architecture and furnishings in the space?

Almost every finely detailed, professionally designed interior includes some touch of Asian influence. These guestroom walls were inspired by the delicate, hand-painted beauty of ancient Chinese watercolor painting on raw silk. The wall mural, though bursting with color and detail, is significantly softened and subdued with a sage-green glaze.

MATERIALS LIST

Square-tipped "bright" and round artist's brushes; 2-inch (51mm) chip brushes; calligraphy brushes; long-haired detail brush; ¾-inch (19mm) nap roller; a sponge roller; steel ticking roller; strié brush; disposable palette; oil glazing liquid; mineral spirits

Sherwin Williams Palette: 1. Ibis White 2. Creamery 3. Decisive Yellow 4. Dishy Coral 5. Exuberant Pink 6. Determined Orange 7. Heartthrob 8. Antiquity 9. Sassy Green 10. Peristyle Brass 11. Ruskin Room Green 12. Dried Thyme 13. Shamrock 14. Hyper Blue 15. Cardboard 16. Smokey Topaz 17. Portabello 18. French Roast 19. Black of Night

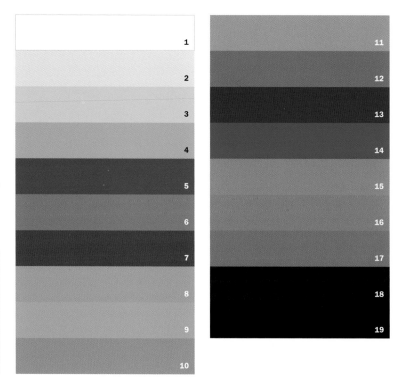

SATIN APPEAL

Satin latex paint is ideal for murals. It moves easily across the basecoat and dries to an attractive sheen.

1 Basecoat the walls. Always begin any mural on a properly prepared surface. Make sure the walls are as smooth as possible, patching or sanding as needed, then apply two coats of a latex paint with an eggshell or satin sheen (here, Benjamin Moore 2165-50). I prefer using a ¾-inch (19mm) nap roller when applying basecoats for a uniform finish.

2 Block in the hills. After the basecoat dries, block in the hilly foreground area with latex satin wall paint in shades of green, yellow, blue and black using a 2-inch (51mm) chip brush and a damp rag. (The colors mix as they're applied.) Spray your working area with water, then begin to define the curve of the hills using a green tone and working from the background to the foreground. As a rule, paint the background detail lighter, darkening the color as you move to the foreground detail. This creates the illusion of depth in the mural. To define the hills, gradually layer the other colors, blending the colors wet-on-wet, and shading according to the direction of any natural light source. Add warm highlights, allowing them to drift over the darker shades.

4 Paint the leaves. When painting the leaves, try to suggest a mass in the background, with more detailed leaves in the foreground. Establish a variety of leaves, quickly sketching leafy shapes using a thinned, midtone green. The paint dries quickly, so immediately begin distinct foreground leaves with stronger tones, giving the closest ones a more defined shape and veining. The leaves in the foreground should have defined highlights and shading. The highlighted side can be wiped with a damp rag to reveal some of the background base color, creating a nice highlight tone. Apply the veining squiggles using a long-haired, artist's detail brush.

INFINITE COLOR

As I introduce colors into a mural, I simply add a dollop of each to my paint-pan palette, letting the colors bleed into each other. Before I know it, I have a wide range of colors to select from. Sometimes I have two, or even three, paint-pan palettes going at the same time. I always use clear disposable inserts, which make for easy clean-up. I usually limit my palette to less than 20 colors per mural, but I can get an infinite range of tones with this type of "mixing."

3 Paint the trees. Lightly sketch the larger trees with thinned brown using square-tipped artist's brushes. Move quickly to establish the general shape of the trunk and limbs, removing mistakes or awkward brushstrokes with a damp rag as you go. Fill in the sketched outline with a watery, medium gray-brown. To shade the trunk, double-load the brush with both the thinned brown and black, then apply the color to the trunk and limbs. Apply the paint more heavily to the shaded side, and lighten the pressure on the brush as you curve the stroke toward the highlighted side. Vary the height and thickness of the trees and branches around the room to balance the design.

5 Block in and define detail objects. First apply a base tone to define the detail's shape, then blend in a darker tone for shading and a lighter tone for highlights. Pay attention to any natural light source entering the room, so you can place the lights and darks naturally. Since this is not a trompe l'oeil mural, keep the painting simple, suggesting detail, rather than painting every single element realistically.

6 Add the stones. To break up the "flatness" of the scene, lightly block in a few stones using a light, diluted tone—anything from brown-gray to pink-peach. Heavily load a square-tipped artist's brush with this watery tone. Place the brush at the top of the blocked-in rock and apply pressure so that the paint is pressed from the bristles and streaks down the wall to create interesting edges. Blot the excess and drips with a rag.

7 Outline the mural elements. Once you're satisfied with the composition, outline the mural element using a Chinese calligraphy brush and—instead of the traditional black ink—watered-down black latex paint. Vary the pressure of the strokes to achieve a random flow of tone. Even if you don't actually replicate the delicate precision of Chinese artwork, it's still fun to try.

8 **Add silk-like texture**. After painting the various elements of the mural, add the silk-like texture. Select a latex paint close to the overall tone you are trying to achieve, but darker than the strié finish you will apply on top. Place a dollop into a disposable palette. Spread the paint out evenly, then gently roll the ticker (a tool used in wood graining) through it until it is evenly coated. Starting at the top, slowly roll the ticker down the wall so that the hatch marks cover the mural. When the paint starts to thin, reload the ticker (you may have to do this often). Skip an area here and there, or randomly roll the ticker in both directions (especially around the edges) to suggest the antiquity of the silk-like surface.

9 **Distress the edge.** When the silk-like texture is dry, distress the ceiling edge of the mural by watering down several tones (in this case, Ruskin Room Green, Peristyle Brass and Cardboard). Doubleload a 2-inch (51mm) chip brush with these tones. Starting at the top of the wall, lightly mist your work area; and then, apply the paint heavily near the ceiling edge. Spray the paint with water so it runs down the wall. Immediately follow with a couple more layers, applying them on top of each other so they mix and layer randomly to create a stained effect. Clean up any unwanted drips with a rag.

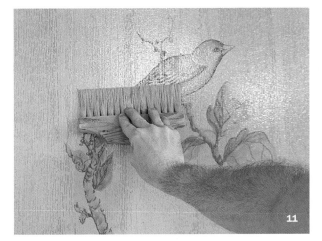

10 **Glaze the wall.** To add a strié finish, mix an oil glaze using 3 parts oil glazing liquid and one part mineral spirits. Add an oil-based tint (here, Ruskin Room Green) to the mix. When the glaze is satisfactory, roll it onto the walls using a sponge roller. Work in sections so that you can strié while the glaze is still wet.

11 **Strié the glaze.** Start at the top and slowly drag a strié brush down the wall. You probably won't reach the bottom comfortably, so stop as close to the base as possible, then position the brush at the base and strié upwards, blending into the previously striated area.

By glazing the mural, the vibrant colors are significantly subdued. The subtle strié finish adds a convincing silky, thread-like texture, and also serves as a durable, protective sealant.

ENTERTAIN THE EYE

I painted the entire mural following this format: block in the shape, define the detail, soften certain areas with watery washes to suggest atmosphere and to add dimension. Unlike a trompe l'oeil mural—where shadows, depth of field and perspective are critical concerns—this is a purely decorative mural. With its focus on elaborate pattern, color and texture, this chinoiserie-inspired mural "entertains" the eye instead of "fooling" it (as trompe l'oeil murals are designed to do).

SYMBOLIC ELEMENTS OF THE MURAL

In Chinese culture, nature is celebrated; and specific native flowers and animals hold significant symbolic and spiritual meaning. Since this mural was especially designed with guests in mind, I included several details to infuse the room with good fortune.

1. The Rabbit. The rabbit is a figure in the Chinese zodiac. People born in the Year of the Rabbit have a lot of good traits—they are said to be intelligent, intuitive, gracious, kind, loyal, sensitive to beauty, diplomatic and peace-loving.
2. The Crane. The crane has an exceptionally long life span, which is undoubtedly why it is used to symbolize longevity. In China, the legendary crane is said to carry the souls of the departed to the heavens. **3. The Butterfly.** In Chinese culture, the butterfly represents love. Flitting from flower to flower, it signifies a happy social life for both the young and young at heart. **4. The Phoenix.** The mythical phoenix is revered in China because of its association with good fortune, virtue, compassion, loyalty and opportunity. Because it is said to rise from its own ashes, it is also associated with resilience.

Italian Tole Sconces.
One of my all-time favorite finds, this pair of floral tole sconces arrived covered in a fresh coat of gold paint. I transformed them with ordinary house paint and a few artist's brushes.

The Magpie.
According to superstition, if a magpie nests in a house, it will bring cause for celebration. It is associated with the joys of family and children.

Flora. The trees in this mural are mostly imaginary, inspired by whatever bright-blooming, twisty trees I could dream up. I tried to create a balance of tall and shorter trees and to give each species a distinctive shape—some corkscrew, some straight, and some with spreading branches.

The guestroom's curved picture window was in similar condition to the one in the dining room. The precious, original panes were cracked, and the wooden frames were in dire need of cosmetic improvement.

My stained-glass artist friend and I have always wanted to collaborate on a project where the window becomes an extension of the surrounding mural. This proved to be the perfect opportunity, as the window is exactly centered opposite the entry to the room. I planned the placement of the lower branches to coincide with the flow of imagery onto the stained glass. To inspire the window design, I simply sketched the placement of the limbs on the old glass with a felt-tip marker. Dave Ehrnschwender defined the details, eventually piecing together the puzzle into this unique architectural showpiece. The bottom panes have a border of odd, purplish glass, while the insets are brilliantly decorated with blossoming branches and even a hand-painted feathered friend. Though this leaded window is more subtle than others in the house, it adds enough whimsy and detail to complete the setting.

Visual Continuity. (Above and at right.) Notice how the flowering branches look as if they not only continue onto the window, but onto the embroidered silk fabric above as well. This visual continuity allows the surrounding wall mural to blend effortlessly. The results are not only visually interesting, but uniquely suited to this guestroom.

The guestroom is furnished with an eclectic mix of furniture and accessories: a Victorian cast-iron bed, a carved Gothic throne chair, an Empire-style cupboard topped with black marble, a pair of French-style bird's-eye maple commodes, a cast iron Victorian cherub lamp, an early Victorian porcelain portrait collection, and so on. The pieces work together, mainly because of the shared palette in the various wood tones, fabrics and accessories. The mood of the room is much lighter and softer than the rest of the house; but even here, the light palette is balanced by the heavy tones in the wood furnishings and iron bed.

As you look over the room, notice how the various fabrics compliment each other. Fine, embellished silks look right at home among the vintage velvet scraps and highly polished printed cotton. Even the simple needlepoint pillow, with its tasseled trimming and tea-stained palette, seems in place.

A Graceful Arrangement. (Above) The graceful arrangement of these pieces brings the decor to life. A guest would be inclined to look at them and wonder about the stories behind them. The intricate details and subtle colors blend beautifully with the room.

Portraits. (Above) The collection of hand-painted, porcelain portraits is a recent acquisition. Portraits add a sense of life and history to a room, as if it has a story to tell.

Cherubic Light. (Right) This Victorian cast-iron lamp, with its delicate, colored, frosted globe, seems made for this room.

COLOR IS KEY

I always decorate with things I love, regardless of their "appropriateness." I focus on color, shape, texture and usefulness when purchasing items. For me, the challenge in decorating is to throw an odd color or shape into the mix of a well-balanced room, then arranging the accessories and furnishings around it. The key to a finely decorated interior is color harmony regardless of style, texture or pattern of the assembled pieces.

ANTIQUED GESSO FINISH

This grand mantelpiece was assembled from several items: the original mantel from the front parlor, new fluted wooden columns, and a French trumeau mirror with a gesso finish. The added height from the mirror makes the fireplace more proportionate to the ten foot ceilings. To unify this combination of pieces, I carried a faux version of the mirror's original gesso finish down to the mantel and wooden columns. To emphasize the beautiful, carved decoration on the mantel, I carefully applied gold leaf; to match it to the gild on the mirror, I distressed it slightly to dull its brilliant brassy surface.

The mantel surround was tiled with a vintage-looking, tumbled-marble mosaic. The tiny floret pattern of the mosaic picks up the floral motif threaded through the house. Completing the fireplace, the hearth is composed of stamped and stained concrete.

MATERIALS LIST

Square-tipped bright brush; gesso; sandpaper; 2-inch (51mm) chip brush; water; strié brush; rags; Imitation Dutch Metal; Wunda Size sizing; cotton balls; Ronan Aqua Leaf bronze/ metallic paint

Sherwin Williams Palette: 1. Nomadic Desert **2.** Portabello **3.** Warm Stone

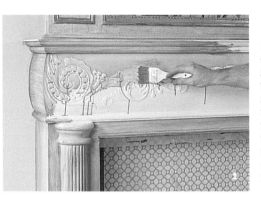

1 Apply gesso and begin antiquing.
Using a 2-inch (51mm) chip brush, apply the gesso thickly, following the direction of the wood grain. Don't smooth out the brushstrokes; you want the surface to be as textured as possible. When this dries, apply a second coat in the same manner. Let dry thoroughly.

Water down several "dirtied" latex colors (I used Nomadic Desert, Warm Stone and Portabello) to stain the gesso. Using a 2-inch (51mm) chip brush, streak the colored wash over the gesso in the direction of the brushstrokes. The color will settle into the fine lines of the brush marks. Continue layering washes, building up darker, dirtied tones around the edges and crevices of the raised details.

2 Add more texture. The trumeau mirror has a definite streaky appearance. To capture this on the mantel, combine the dirtied tones to form an antique-colored wash and quickly apply it using a 2-inch (51mm) chip brush. Immediately follow with a swipe of the strié brush, leaving a more defined, linear texture.

3 Distress the finish. Once you're satisfied with the "antiquity" of the tone, lightly sand the mantel following the direction of the brushstrokes. This will bring the gesso's texture back to the surface, creating a subtly worn but clean look.

4 Prepare for gilding. Wipe the mantel thoroughly with a soft cloth to remove any residue from the sanding. Next, apply sizing to the areas where gold leaf will be applied.

ALL THAT GLITTERS...

For gilding, I usually use sheets of inexpensive, brass Imitation Dutch Metal. It's just as lovely as the 23K gold, and significantly less expensive.

5 **Gild the mantel.** After the sizing is almost dry, but still slightly tacky, gently tamp the sheets of gold leaf over the sizing with a soft-bristled artist's brush. To ensure adhesion, burnish the gilded areas with a cotton ball. The excess gold leaf should become brittle and break away. When all the gilding is complete, vacuum the loose particles from the mantel.

6 **Soften the gold leaf.** The gold leaf can appear very harsh. To tone it down to match the gilding on the mirror, I applied an antiquing color wash (Warm Stone) over the gilded areas. I let the wash dry for a minute or so, then gently wiped the surface with a soft rag, leaving most of the color around the edges.

Balance Through Contrast. This Gothic throne chair, a housewarming gift from friends who sell antiques, is from the nineteenth-century. The burgundy and gold brocade upholstery, however, is recent and gives the chair a fresh lease on life. I'm particularly fond of the chair's height. It has an almost sculptural quality in this otherwise soft setting. The dark, heavily carved chair sits next to the light, almost dainty fireplace, balancing it through contrast.

7 **Splatter the surface.** Using the watered-down colors from step 1 (Nomadic Desert, Warm Stone and Portabello), splatter the mantel. To splatter color, load a 2-inch (51mm) chip brush or an old toothbrush with the thinned paint, then run your fingers across the bristles. This will cause fine specks of color—resembling particles of dust or grime—to spray across the surface.

8 **Age the cast-iron surround.** To give the cast-iron surround an appealing presence and bring out its lovely floral details, lightly drybrush the raised decoration with acrylic gold paint (I used Ronan Aqua Leaf, which is water-based and combines bronze and Aztec gold colors). Using a square-tipped "bright" brush, drybrush the darker bronze first, then follow with a more brilliant gold to highlight the most pronounced area of the decoration.

9 **Soften the drybrushing.** To give the cast iron a dusty, hazy effect, apply a wash of Warm Stone.

10 **Remove excess color.** Wipe the raised areas with a soft rag before it dries completely, leaving most of the color in the crevices.

Let dry, then seal the mantel and cast-iron surround with polyurethane. (Imitation Dutch metal must be sealed, or it will tarnish over time.)

Fireplace Before. (Above) Before the fauxing is complete, the fireplace pieces seem like individual elements, not a cohesive whole.

Comforting With Texture. The billowing window shades (which can be easily lowered for privacy) are made from raw silk and covered with delicate, hand-embroidered vines, adding a three-dimensional texture to the room. The nineteenth-century, cast-iron bed is dressed with a shimmering silk coverlet. The tone-on-tone look of the fabrics, walls and flooring (the acanthus carpeting was less costly than hardwood) gives the room a comforting and calming influence.

Since the guest bathroom is located across the hall from the guestroom, I chose to coordinate the spaces by expanding on the garden theme. I applied an atmospheric, tone-on-tone color wash to enliven the narrow room. This faux finish makes small areas feel larger, especially when the finish is continued onto the ceiling. I used the color wash as a background for a rambling cabbage rose, which climbs from below the pedestal sink, up the wall, and across the ceiling. To emphasize the projecting window wall, I applied a faux-weathered-concrete finish, continuing it across to the rear wall, as well. The effect is perfect for an area like this: Not only does it have an old, garden-wall feel, but it also breaks up the different planes in the room, adding architectural interest.

Bathroom Before. The guest bathroom was a dingy, cramped wreck. I gutted the room and started over.

Vintage Light. (Above) I purchased a wonderful vintage chandelier, made in Italy, from an online auction site, then painted it to match the shower tiles. I sprayed the entire chandelier with B-I-N primer, then brushed the leaves with green (Privilege Green) and the roses with yellow (June Day). I sprayed the centers of the roses with pink spray paint for added detail. For the final warm tone, I lightly drybrushed the entire chandelier pale yellow (Friendly Yellow).

The Perfect Palette. (Right) The glazed-porcelain tiles in the shower have a faded, fresco appeal. The warm yellow-orange patina of the checker-board border adds the perfect amount of color to the neutral field tiles. The dark bronze plumbing fixtures contrast beautifully with the soft, light palette.

Bathroom After. The room is furnished with a solid, cast-iron, architectural salvage piece. Other than adding a wash of color to dress it up, I left the piece as it was. The rusted patina makes it look like it's naturally weathered from leaning against a water-stained concrete wall for years. I purchased it at a local open-air antiques market, along with the scalloped, honey-pine mirror. I especially admire the mirror's distressed finish. The bits of white paint remnants over the pine suggest the same finishes used in the guestroom fireplace. The amber, hand-blown Venetian vases and delicately sculpted glass butterflies are treasured souvenirs from a trip to the island of Murano in Venice, Italy. Completing the setting is a pair of black framed vintage botanical prints hanging near the walk-in shower entrance.

RAMBLING ROSE MURAL

One of the most rewarding aspects of my career as a decorative artist is watching a room blossom into life with paint. A well-executed mural can transform the drab to the dazzling—warming the ambiance of even the most barren room. This rather insignificant, narrow guest bathroom, for example, has been totally transformed into a serene and placid garden paradise.

The transformation began with a soft, cloud-like color wash. The effect from this simple painting technique is significant, as it creates the strong illusion of space in a room, especially one as confining as this. On top of this atmospheric color, an old-fashioned cabbage rose twines toward the ceiling. A pair of textured, faux-concrete walls wear a weathered patina, suggesting years of exposure to the elements.

MATERIALS LIST

2-inch (51mm) chip brushes; square-tipped and round artist's brushes; spray bottle; joint compound; paint roller; rags; sand

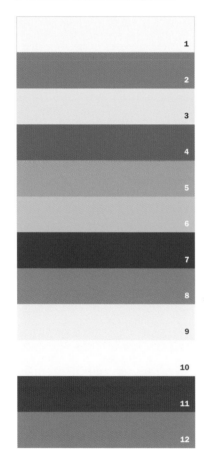

Sherwin Williams Palette: 1. Friendly Yellow 2. Privilege Green 3. June Day 4. Tea Chest 5. Tony Taupe 6. Torch Light 7. Poinsettia 8. Grenadine 9. Jersey Cream 10. Antique White 11. Coconut Husk 12. Chamois

1 **Apply basecoat.** To emphasize the window wall and its adjoining back wall, I applied a trompe l'oeil weathered-concrete finish. To do this, mix a couple of handfuls of sand into about a gallon (4 liters) of joint compound. Add about a half cup (118ml) of gray latex satin paint (here, Tony Taupe) to give it the perfect consistency for rolling on with a roller. The mixture's rough texture is a good imitation of the pitted feel of real concrete. Let dry.

2 **Add water-streaked look.** Create a water-streaked appearance using several shades of color (here, Tea Chest, Torchlight and Tony Taupe). Dip a 2-inch (51mm) chip brush in water and pick up one or several colors. Deposit the color near the ceiling, then spray with water so the paint runs down the wall. Mix the colors wet-on-wet for best effect.

3 **Paint the remaining walls.** Basecoat the remaining walls with Antique White. Using a 2-inch (51mm) chip brush, apply a two-color wash (here, Chamois and Jersey Cream). Spray a working area, dip the brush in water, pick up some color and scrub it around. Don't overwork the wash—it's best to get the random flow going first, then darken areas here and there after it has dried.

4 **Blend brushstrokes.** To blend as many brushstrokes as possible, feather out the color into the surrounding areas using a dry, 2-inch (51mm) chip brush.

5 **Add vining roses.** Freehand paint a rambling cabbage rose vine along the parchment-like walls. Start by painting the vines, then add the leaves and finally the rose clusters using the pinks and greens and browns listed and square-tipped and round artist's brushes. (Small details like this can add a lot of punch to a small space. Vines, in particular, are ideal for directing the eye away from the toilet or architectural defects within a space.)

Rose Clusters. (Above) Clusters of pink cabbage roses flourish against the "sun-drenched" color wash of the background.

Old-World Style. (Right) Reflected in the scalloped, honey-pine mirror is a small towel niche conveniently tucked next to the shower. The bronze fixtures add an old-world flavor to the vintage-style pedestal sink.

THE LAUNDRY ROOM

The laundry room is nestled at the rear of the hall that leads to the third-floor master suite. The room proved to be a challenge because it houses not only a noisy washer and dryer, but the third-floor heating system as well. To help sound-proof the environment, my apprentice Robin Harrison recommended a product called JaDécor. JaDécor is composed of dyed cotton particles and cellulose, with anything from colored metallic threads to mica, added to customize the look to suit any décor. It arrives in dry form and is then mixed with warm water and troweled onto the wall.

JaDécor has many advantages. It resembles a beautiful, seamless, hand-made paper surface when dry and can be easily customized by adding fabric dyes. It insulates against noise and extreme temperature change and is not affected by humidity, making it ideal to use in the laundry room. JaDécor is also a "green" building product, meaning it's ranked as one of the safest and most environmentally friendly wall coverings on the market.

RESOURCES

JaDécor Wall Covering
E-mail: info@jadecor.com
Website: www.jadecor.com
Phone: 1-888-677-3642

MATERIALS LIST

JaDécor; trowel; trough; large plastic tub; water; plastic garbage bag for mixing; KILZ premium sealer; bonding paint (or ceiling paint, joint compound, and pearlite); paint roller; paint pan

1 Assemble the ingredients. Assemble your materials, then prepare the walls with KILZ Premium sealer to create a water barrier. Next, apply a coat of bonding paint. You can purchase this or you can make it yourself (mix 1 gallon [4 liters] latex ceiling paint, 1 cup [237ml] joint compound and 2 cups [474ml] pearlite). The bonding paint gives a slight texture that the JaDécor can adhere to.

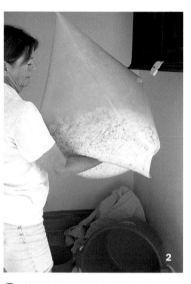

2 Mix the ingredients. Mix the ingredients in a large, clear plastic bag. Robin simply rotated and shook the mixture until the ingredients were uniformly dispersed.

3 Add water. Slowly add warm water. Using your bare hands, thoroughly mix the materials.

4 Trowel on JaDécor. Once thoroughly mixed, place a working amount of JaDécor on a trough, and trowel the mixture onto the wall. Working from the ceiling down, apply the mixture in a thin, even coat (much like icing a cake). JaDécor dries completely in about two or three days. The material will get significantly lighter in color as the moisture evaporates form the product.

Making the Most of the Limited Space.
The washer and dryer are neatly stacked
in the corner near the furnace, making the most of the limited space. The
second-floor location is much more
convenient than the long trip to the basement laundry room. Notice how the mica
and copper threads sparkle in the sun-lit
atmosphere.

Practical but Attractive. (Right) The faux-
grained cupboard (circa early 1800s) was
one of my earliest acquisitions. It has
followed me through several residences.
Originally, the top piece was attached, but
I removed it to create a surface for fold-
ing. I restored the graining on the door
panels, which had lost its detail over the
years, with yellowing varnish. The lidded
jars hold detergent, softener sheets and
some sweets (to motivate me to get the
laundry done).

The Power of Color

Using color is the easiest way to personalize your home—and the least understood. Maybe that's why so many of us are content to live in a "neutral" world. Color, though easy to apply, is difficult to choose, even for the professional (it took me several tries to get the study's base color). Between the base color, the accent colors, and the incidental colors, there are enough decisions in the mix to send people dashing right back into their neutral—and often boring—comfort zone.

As an artist, I can't imagine living in a colorless environment. Color comforts me, seduces me, warms me, surprises me, and foremost, inspires me. This home, though grounded with an earthy Tuscan palette (golden amber, olive greens and terracotta), celebrates saturated color with accents of cobalt, emerald, ruby, teal, orange and even lime green.

When trying to figure out a color scheme for clients, I always "borrow" from their favorite work of art, or the colors in their wardrobes. Examine your surroundings, and study the things that capture your attention: Is there a common thread, a particular color, vibrancy or combination of tones? The answer to your color dilemma is most likely right in front of you!

1. and 2. Accent Color. The beaded tassel in the parlor inspired the overall palette for my home. From here, I introduced richly colored finishes and furniture into the décor. The books, candlestick, and even the brilliant, rich blue of Mary's cloak in the antique lithograph relate to the vibrant colors in the simple tassel. **3. Saturated Color.** The bold colors of the sunlit glass and the saturated hues of the painting relax the otherwise "serious" study. I found this unusual, lime-green penguin in—of all places—a Kentucky hay field along Route 127 during the famed "World's Longest Yard Sale." The solid glass sculpture was extremely heavy, so I left the penguin in the car while I explored other vendors. When I came back an hour later, the blazing August sun had filtered through the penguin, burning a hole in the seat! **4. Fanciful Flights of Color.** These vintage collectibles feature bold tropical colors and bring a smile to a guest's face. The birds in this collection personalized the otherwise uninteresting nook in the second floor hallway. **5. Tropical Color.** I carried the tropical bird theme into the nearby laundry room; the lovely colors of their plumage make an irresistible accent.

MASTER SUITE

THE WONDERFUL THING about older homes is all the little unexpected nooks and crannies that add so much fun and interest to the interior architecture. The third-floor master suite is just that type of space—full of awkward angles, sloping walls and unexpected surprises! And many of those surprises were hidden away under tons of clutter and crumbling plaster walls.

Originally serving as a dumping ground for the previous owners, the third floor now boasts a luxurious master suite, complete with a graceful cathedral ceiling; a spacious, custom-built, walk-in closet; a deluxe master bath; and an intimate, yet functional art studio area.

Master Suite Before. The original space was so crammed with clutter, that it was impossible to walk from one end of the room to the other. **Master Suite During Demolition.** Once the clutter and plaster were cleared out, the room's potential became more obvious. **Master Suite After Construction.** To use as much of the rather awkward space as possible, I decided to install custom cabinets into the knee wall areas flanking the huge center window.

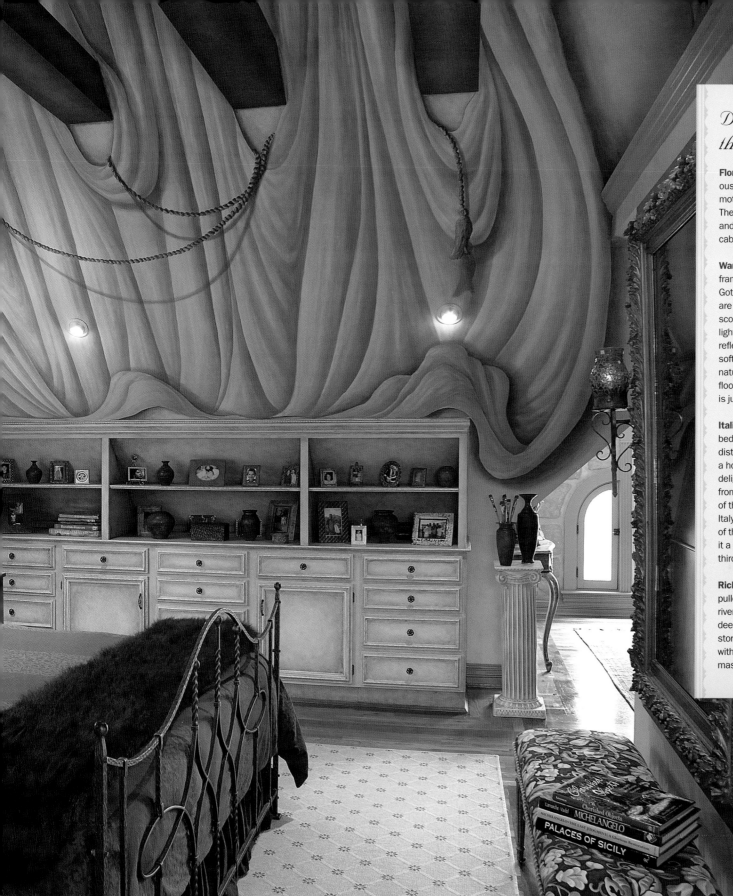

Details Define the Setting

Floral motif. Though not as obvious as in the guestroom, the floral motif has a place in this room too. The small red florets in the carpet and the blossom-shaped iron cabinet knobs play to that theme.

Warm light. The ornate gold frame of the mirror reinforces the Gothic motif. Flanking the mirror are two glittering, glass-mosaic sconces. Their warm, orange light sparkles in the glass and reflects off the mirror, bringing a soft brightness to the room. The natural light is limited on the third floor, and this quiet, intimate light is just what the room needs.

Italian Gothic. I ordered the iron bed with its Gothic lines and distressed gunmetal finish from a home décor magazine. To my delight, the bed was imported from Italy. Considering how much of the home's décor is inspired by Italy, it seemed fated. The weight of the wrought-iron frames made it a challenge to get up to the third floor!

Rich stone. Where the drapery is pulled back, it reveals the wall of river stone hiding beneath. The deep, rich colors in the painted stones balance and harmonize with the real slate dominating the master bath.

RAG-TEXTURED FINISH

The trompe l'oeil drapery needed a solid background to support it. I decided to keep it simple with an elegant rag-textured faux finish. This finish can be easily applied with any group of colors (any more than four colors, however, begins to look too busy). I decided to limit myself to three paints: a warm, buttery tan (Harvester); Spearmint; and Antique White for the base color. These colors contrast with the yellow-gold drapes and offset the darker tones of the wood and stones. Having a textured background color allows me to paint the drapery's shadows, where as an atmospheric background wouldn't. Painting a shadow goes a long way to helping the illusion.

MATERIALS LIST

rags; water; spray bottle; paint pan; 2-inch (51mm) chip brush (for use around corners); ¾-inch (19mm) nap roller

Sherwin Williams Palette: 1. Harvester 2. Antique White 3. Spearmint

1 Mottle the color. Apply an Antique White basecoat, with a ¾-inch (19mm) nap roller. A high-quality paint with a satin finish is a good base for faux finishes because it doesn't absorb the washes, allowing you more time to manipulate the finish. Place a dollop of each paint color (Harvester and Spearmint) in corners of a disposable paint pan. Spray a working area of the wall with water. Pick up a small amount of Spearmint on a damp rag and scrub it onto the wall. Do this with Harvester, mottling the two colors together using a crumpled rag while the paint is still damp.

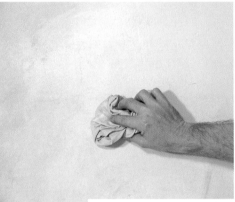

2 Balance the color. Keep adding and blending the tones until a soft, atmospheric texture emerges. To balance out the two colors, use a damp rag to mottle in some of the Antique White base color where needed.

Wait until the paint is dry before deepening or softening an area for a uniform finish. If the area is still wet, you will lift the paint, creating bald areas that can be difficult to conceal. Concentrate on pattern and an evenly textured appearance.

Elements of a Scene.
This carved chest of drawers stores painting supplies, as well as a few renderings. The Japanese-influenced silk needlepoint on the wall was a stunning find at an antiques mall. The antique parlor chair is carved with griffins, bringing a perfect touch of the Gothic theme into this corner of the room. The twisting acanthus leaf shows up here, too, in the table lamp.

FAUX RIVER-STONE FINISH

To balance out the heavy, rich color in the slate master bath, I applied a rounded river stone look to the main wall behind the bed and in the gabled wall in the art studio. This was an easy look to achieve, and the results are fairly realistic. Practically any natural tones found in stone may be used and still fit with any decor.

A Welcome Update. The windows in the exterior gables had been covered by aluminum siding. I replaced the old, drafty windows with new, high-efficiency windows.

MATERIALS LIST

Joint compound; 1½- to 3-inch (38mm to 75mm) putty knives; latex paint; rags; 2-inch (51mm) chip brushes; ¼- to 1½-inch (6mm to 38mm) square-tipped artist's brushes; colored chalk; water; 220-grit sandpaper; spray bottle; polyurethane

Sherwin Williams Palette: 1. Arresting Auburn 2. Storm Cloud 3. Tricorn Black 4. Plum Dandy 5. Butternut 6. Believable Buff 7. Red Cent 8. Revel Blue

1 Sketch and texture the stones.
Using colored chalk, sketch a pattern of stones to fit the space. Leave grout areas between the stones for added realism.

To establish the texture and base color of the stones, tint a workable amount of joint compound with a dollop of light brown (or other color of your choosing) latex paint. Using a putty knife, place about a ¼-inch (6mm) bead of the tan-tinted joint compound on the edge of the blade and press it gently onto the chalk line, then drag towards the center. Leave irregular edges and areas free of compound to capture the true texture of stone.

2 Shade the grout. When the joint compound dries, shade the grout areas. Place a dollop of brown (Arresting Auburn), black (Tricorn Black), and grey (Storm Cloud) in a paint tray. Let them mix together. Dip your brush in water and then randomly pick up color. Apply a shadow under and to the right or left of each stone, according to any natural light source in the room.

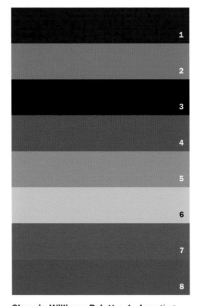

3 Paint the stone. Using a spray bottle, lightly mist the individual stones and blend several shades together for a natural look. I used latex satin paint in the following tones: grey (Storm Cloud), blue (Revel Blue), rust (Red Cent), brown (Arresting Auburn), tan (Believable Buff), purple (Plum Dandy), ochre (Butternut) and black (Tricorn Black). Place a dollop of each color on a disposable paint tray, then pick up any color on a 1 ½-inch (38mm) square-tipped artist's brush and scrub the color into the stones. Blend colors together with a damp rag if needed. You can also use the damp rag to lift color from the center of some stones for added realism. Simply scrub the center to create a "halo" effect.

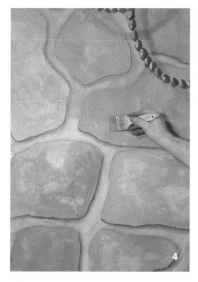

4 **Tint the wall.** To deepen and "cool" down the overall tone of the stone, apply a latex color wash over the entire wall. Mix about a cup of the grey tone (Storm Cloud), with about a half cup (118mL) of water. Starting at the top, brush this wash over the wall with a 2-inch (51mm) chip brush.

5 **Soften the wash.** Have a damp rag handy to spread and soften the wash, and to catch any drips. You want the wash to be as evenly applied as possible.

6 **Reinforce the shadows and sand.** Darken some of the shadows beneath and next to the stones, using the same tones as in step 2.

To give the stone's patina an interesting appearance, lightly sand each stone with 220-grit sandpaper. Don't oversand, especially around the edges, or a definite, unnatural outline will appear. Wipe down the walls, then seal with polyurethane.

The Stones Revealed. For added interest, I knotted the fabric on one side, as if it was tied back to reveal the rich river stones hiding behind the curtain. Someday, I might paint the suggestion of a figure or two peeking from behind.

The night stand/chest is the first piece of furniture I ever painted. Though it was completed 20 years ago, it fits perfectly with the room's decor. Just imagine—I purchased the original chest at an auction for ten dollars!

MASTER BEDROOM TROMPE L'OEIL DRAPES

The wonderful thing about painted drapery is how dramatically the swooping folds and cascading, tasseled roping can transform a space. Married with a cathedral ceiling, the impact is remarkable. The fun aspect of painted drapery is the creative freedom it allows; the fabric is custom-shaped, gathered and tucked to conform to the architectural limitations of the room. The folds can be softened with the addition of dangling double roping, accented with oversized tassels. As with real fabric, painted drapery can be gathered as if it's hanging from a rod, or—for a more formal appearance—pleated as if held in place with decorative hardware.

Painting drapery is not as difficult as it may appear. Once the positioning of the fabric is established, it helps to drape a real drop cloth or similar piece of fabric to imitate the look you wish to achieve and to note the way the shadows and highlights fall on the surface. Using a basic midtone combined with a highlight and shadow tone brings the painted drapery magically to life.

THE RIGHT BRUSH FOR THE JOB

A square-tipped, 1-inch (25mm) flat artist's brush is perfect for this job. Its shape will help you keep the paint inside the individual fold lines.

MATERIALS LIST

Colored chalk; water; palette knife; ¼- to 1½-inch (6mm to 38mm) square-tipped artist's brushes; paint pan; water

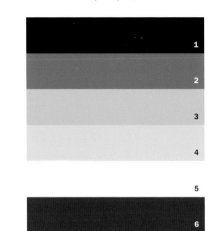

Sherwin Williams Palette: 1. Tricorn Black 2. Saucy Gold 3. Sunrise 4. Jonquil 5. Dover White 6. Turkish Coffee

1 Sketch the drape pattern. Sketch the fabric using easily erasable colored chalk. Having the cathedral ceilings to play with here, I knew I wanted the fabric to be lush with deep folds and lots of movement, especially as the fabric nears the beams. The gathered drapery above the cabinets looks as if it has been pulled back to reveal the contents on the shelves.

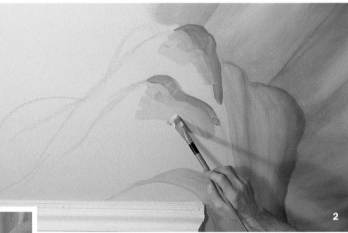

2 Begin shading. Paint the drapes' base color using a medium tone latex house paint in a color you'd like to emphasize in the room. I used a combination of two deep, golden colors—Jonquil and Sunrise—to establish my base tone. Use a square-tipped artist's brush to define the individual folds of the drape.

Start at the top of the wall and work your way down. After blocking in the base tone, shade by blending Saucy Gold into the base color, followed with a Dover White highlight on the right. Concentrate on individual folds instead of the entire wall area at once. Continue painting down and across the wall until you've achieved the general feel of drapery.

3 Add shadows to the drape. To add dimension to the folds, add brown and black to your palette. Mix the two colors, thinning the mixture with water to create a translucent glaze. Use this glaze and a 1-inch (25mm) square-tipped artist's brush to paint a thin shadow under the folds of the fabric, on the wall under the drape, and anywhere a shadow would fall naturally according to the natural lighting in the room. To achieve the desired depth, you may need to apply several layers. Let the first coat dry before doing so.

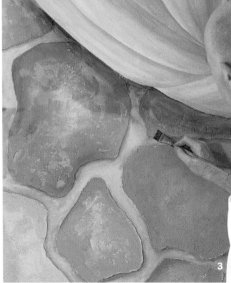

4 **Add highlights.** At this point, a hint of light bouncing from one side of the drape should already be established. The idea here is to emphasize how any natural light entering the room would fall upon the drapery. Add a little white to your palette, and combined with the highlight tone (Dover White), brush a gentle hint of natural light on one side of the drape folds. Feather out the brushstrokes, by softly brushing back and forth.

Personal Comfort. Master bedrooms should evoke personal comfort, and that's exactly what this trompe l'oeil drapery suggests: warm, cozy luxury. The lush drapery folds appear to dangle from an iron rod. In fact, the rod is a PVC pipe spray-painted with a bronze metallic paint, cut to fit, and attached to the cathedral ceiling crest with construction adhesive.

Oliver, my adopted cat, has been part of this house from the beginning. One late summer evening, not long after I bought the house, my brother and I were waterproofing the stone walls in the basement. Oliver jumped through an open window and right onto my back! He was obviously a stray and nearly starving, so I kept him. He regards the third floor as his domain.

TROMPE L'OEIL DRAPERY ROPING

The cascading swags of rope and deep shadows, strengthen the fool-the-eye effect by taking some of the focus off the painted drapery. When you add a contrasting element like this into a trompe l'oeil setting, it seduces the viewer by adding further dimension to the scene. A large shot of this room was featured in a local newspaper article, prior to a home tour I participated in. The number of visitors on the home tour who were stunned to find out the drapery and roping were just paint stunned *me!* The looks of disbelief on their faces were priceless.

MATERIALS LIST

Colored chalk; water; palette knife; joint compound; artist's square-tipped and detail brushes; paint pan

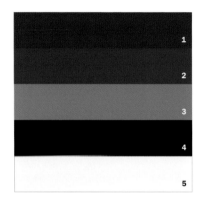

Sherwin Williams Palette: 1. Fireweed 2. Izmir Purple 3. Invigorate 4. Tricorn Black 5. Antique White

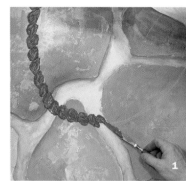

1 **Sculpt the rope.** Begin by sketching the rope with chalk. Experiment with dramatic dips in the design; think of the roping as a artistic tool, instrumental in making the viewer's eye dance about the room. Once you're satisfied with the flow of the roping, add a three-dimensional aspect with joint compound. First, tint the compound with the red paint (Fireweed), then carefully sculpt the relief using a curved palette knife to form the individual swirls in the roping. Although time-consuming, this adds significant dimension.

2 **Shade the rope.** When the compound is dry, shade the rope using the red base color (Fireweed) mixed with purple (Izmir Purple). Shade according to the direction of the light in the room.

3 **Add the lighter tone.** Mix the base color (Fireweed) with orange (Invigorate). Again paying attention to the direction of the light in the room, add the lighter tone.

4 **Add highlights.** You can add some white (Antique White) to the orange mixture to lighten it, or add wisps of white directly to the rope.

5 **Add realistic shadows.** Paint a heavy shadow using a thinned mixture of brown and black. The shadow should emphasize the dramatic sweeps of the rope. In placing the shadow, keep any sources of natural light in the room in mind.

The Tasseled Effect. The roping and oversized tassels' appeal comes from their unusual mix of contrasting colors and their remarkable, three-dimensional, sculpted presence. The combined effect is highly realistic, practically jumping off the golden toned background.

FAUX WOOD RAILROAD TIE BEAMS

The beams in the master bedroom were created by beefing up the original collar ties bridging the rafters with ordinary ¼-inch (6mm) pine plywood. This introduced a more informal look, adding country elegance and additional architectural interest to the room.

The cathedral ceiling draws your attention upward to the beams hovering over the bed. The beams look heavy and oiled, like railroad ties, adding strength to the drapery's soft effect. The beams may seem solid, but they aren't even fully enclosed; I left the top open so that the recessed lighting could be properly vented.

Though similar to the beams in the kitchen, these rafters have no faux graining.

Before. Here, with the plywood "skeleton" waiting for its magical transformation, you can see the ceiling fan I installed. This keeps the hot air circulating and casts a warm amber light that suits the room's ambiance.

MATERIALS LIST

spray bottle; water; 2-inch (51mm) chip brush; small roller; rags

Sherwin Williams Palette: 1. Arresting Auburn 2. Tricorn Black 3. Reynard

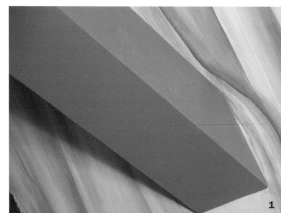

1 **Basecoat the beams.** Apply a basecoat of a rich orange terra-cotta color (Reynard) in latex satin using a small roller.

2 **Antique the beams.** Use a 2-inch (51mm) chip brush and a combination of Tricorn Black and Arresting Auburn to paint the beams. Shade the beam using the two colors double-loaded or mixed. Lightly mist a 4-foot (1m) section of the beam, and scrub the two colors onto the beam with a 2-inch (51mm) chip brush. Soften the shading toward the center, allowing the brilliancy of the base color to glow through.

3 **Emphasize the beams with a halo effect.** Before the paint has completely dried, take a slightly damp rag and scrub it in a circular motion from the center of the beam outward. Rub gently enough to leave the paint in the crevices of the rough plywood. Feather out any remaining rag or brush swirls by lightly drybrushing with a clean 2-inch (51mm) chip brush.

After. The finished beams hover over the room. Though they have the presence of old railroad ties, the beams are actually hollow and constructed of lightweight ¼-inch (6mm) plywood. They lend depth to the faux finish, and their execution allowed me to try some interesting effects with the draping of the faux fabric.

DISTRESSED BUILT-IN CABINETS

Adequate storage space is virtually nonexistent in older homes. Because I look at storage as a necessity rather than a luxury, I was determined to add sufficient storage space to the master bedroom. To maximize as much of the awkward, angled wall as possible, I purchased inexpensive standard-stock bar and kitchen cabinets, pairing them with custom, built-in shelving. The variously sized drawers and cabinets help organize garments, providing more than enough storage for the room.

I finished the cabinets with a warm, mellow patina. I plan to eventually enhance the cabinets with painted detailing in the classical style. This softly patinated, neutral finish is the perfect backdrop for such future embellishment.

MATERIALS LIST

Primer; 2-inch (51mm) chip brush; rags; water; Faux Effects Porcelain Crackle medium; polyurethane

Sherwin Williams Palette: 1. Jute Brown 2. Tatami Tan 3. Spearmint

SEAL THE WOOD

As with most faux finishes applied to unpainted wood, it's advisable to first seal or prime the surface before proceeding.

1 **Seal the bare wood.** Seal the unpainted wood with a coat of primer. To give the built-in cabinets the look of layered paint, I applied a fine porcelain-like crackle with Faux Effects products using the techniques discussed on pages 82-83.

To highlight the delicate, crackled surface, apply a thinned latex glaze made from the light and mid-tone browns. Using a moist 2-inch (51mm) chip brush, pick up a tiny amount of the combined colors. Scrub the glaze heavily around the edges and more softly toward the center. Repeat after first coat dries, further darkening the patina, especially at the edges.

2 **Seal the finish.** While the color is still damp, remove color from the raised areas with a damp rag. Use the damp rag to remove excess color from the center area of the cabinet drawers and doors for a "halo" effect. Rub gently; you want to remove or soften the top color only, not the color in the cracks and intricately carved recesses.

For cabinets and shelving, it's always recommended to seal the paint finish with polyurethane. I suggest two or three coats, with light sanding in between.

Texture Detail. The delicate, beaded, wood trim was applied to the otherwise stock cabinet fronts, adding an old-world charm. The layered, aged finish has just enough dirt to suggest that these cabinets have been in place for years. The blossom-like knob (also used in the studio's wainscoting) continues the floral thread.

After. The gently distressed finish blends beautifully with the draped walls and amber-tinted hardwood floors. Inside the shelving areas, the blue faux finish adds an unexpected but welcome color accent. Delicate, blossom-like hardware with a rusty finish completes the ensemble.

MASTER BATH

When I purchased the house, this room was home to a family of nesting pigeons. They were entering the attic through broken windows, meandering through the maze of rafters into a warm and safe "sanctuary"—that is to say, my master bath.

I spent months trying to remove these persistent characters, who are by nature obnoxiously territorial. I patched every opening I could see in the attic. When I didn't see any more droppings, I knew the pigeons were gone and went to work demolishing the room. It was hot, horrible work and the mess was considerable. After we carried out the last bucket of debris, cleaned the window sills, vacuumed the dust and mopped the floors, it looked presentable enough to invite my bank's loan officer to do a walk-though of the property.

To my horror, we entered the attic and found four of my feathered foes perched in the exposed collar ties... and a minefield of fresh droppings!

It took six more frustrating months to fully evict the vermin from their luxurious aviary. But in memory of the epic battle, I immortalized one of the birds in the master bath. This lone pigeon crouches quietly over the tub, a whimsical reminder of who truly rules the roost!

Master Bath Before. (Left) It takes a practiced, creative eye to recognize that such an odd, cramped space could be anything more than storage.

The Complete Master Bath. (Right) Creating a deluxe master bath was one of the most challenging aspects of the renovation. Because of the odd, angled walls in this area, the whirlpool tub had to be positioned in front of the windows. As an extra indulgence, I installed a built-in wall heater unit in the bath; when turned on, it has a sauna-like effect.

START AT THE TOP

When remodeling, you should always start with the highest floor and work your way down. The soot and grime behind the layers of old plaster and lath is often uncontainable and will thickly blanket the lower floors (along with your lungs, so wear masks!). The soot was particularly bad here because, as the charred lumber under the plaster showed, there must have been a fire in the house.

Rich Slate. The slate tile was irresistible, with its rainbow of rich, natural tones. I designed the placement of field slate at a diagonal for extra visual interest. I'm especially fond of the upper mosaic tiles (which repeat on the floor). The iridescent glow of some of them is amazing, especially when wet.

The warm caramel-toned, Venetian-plastered walls provide the perfect hint of texture. The rich velvety surface contrasts perfectly with the cool slate tones.

A collection of iron candlesticks creates a relaxing atmosphere for soaking in the whirlpool tub.

Stained wooden blinds provide privacy but can be easily opened to flood the south-facing room with wonderful light.

This family of hand-made turtles bear unusual glazed finishes. I purchased them as souvenirs on a trip to Montreal, Canada. I couldn't help putting them in the master bath.

Luxury bath towels sport floral embroidery, carrying the floral motif to the third floor.

The flexible decorative trim was attached with construction adhesive and given a rusted finish. Small details like this add immense old-world charm to a setting.

VENETIAN-PLASTERED WALLS

There are a lot of oddly angled walls in the master bath area. I decided to unify them with a softly textured, tone-on-tone Venetian plaster finish. This simple but physically demanding finish (the application requires a lot of elbow grease, as does the burnishing) is perfect for creating a subtle yet sophisticated look. It has a lovely, fine shimmer that doesn't scream "faux" and also blends elegantly with the woodwork.

This product comes ready-to-apply and requires little or no wall preparation. Behr Venetian plaster is readily available and comes in various colors (no mystery or mixing). The only other tools needed are a flexible, straight-edged steel trowel and a plastic mud pan or plasterer's trough to hold the plaster.

MATERIALS LIST

Behr Venetian plaster (Tuscany Tan); 6-inch (15cm) straight-edged flexible steel trowel; plastic mud pan

Sherwin Williams Palette: 1. Tuscany Tan

A GOOD FINISH

This finish is ideal for areas with odd angles and planes. (With patterns or texture, you often have to worry about matching up the planes.) This tone-on-tone, all-over finish is easy to apply from one plane to the next without noticeable interruption in the flow or application.

1 **Apply the first coat of Venetian plaster.** If the walls are already painted, simply patch any holes or damaged areas. If the walls have never been painted, then prepare them with a primer undercoat before applying the plaster.

Place a workable amount (about 3 cups [71ml]) of Venetian plaster into the mud pan. Lift about a ¼-inch (6mm) bead of plaster onto the flexible steel blade edge. Holding the blade at a 15 to 30 degree angle, spread a thin layer of the plaster back and forth across the wall. It's best to work from the top down. Complete coverage isn't necessary in this step—just aim for an irregularly layered application.

2 **Apply a second coat.** After the first coat has dried (approximately four hours), apply the final coat of Venetian plaster using the same technique as described in step 1; but this time, hold the blade at more of a 60 to 90 degree angle. You can let this layer overlap the edges of the first, but it's meant especially to fill any voids left from the first application. Allow this layer to dry for 24 hours.

3 **Burnish the walls.** (Left) To achieve a highly polished, wax-like appearance, vigorously burnish the dried plaster using the same flexible steel applicator. Forcibly glide the blade across the surface in random directions until the desired luster is achieved. Continue until you're satisfied with the sheen.

STOWAWAY

The angles of the room don't really allow for cabinets or closets, but hooks and cubby holes provide an excellent alternative. Work with the shape of the room, not against it.

MASTER BATH TROMPE L'OEIL WINDOW

I tried to weave a Gothic influence through the house, from the antique church sconces in the hallways, to the arched stained glass windows in the gathering room. The master bath is no exception. Precisely poised above the luxury whirlpool tub, a trompe l'oeil scalloped slate window brings the Gothic influence into this room. The richly textured, velvety impression of the Venetian-plastered walls frames the window well. A lone mourning dove quietly observes the scene, as a trailing vine of ivy cascades in and about the window frame. The cool yet rich dark tones in the slate (both the real slate and the painted), juxtapose brilliantly with the warm, polished walls.

MATERIALS LIST

Joint compound; 1 ½-inch (37mm) putty knife; square-tipped and rounded artist's brushes; artist's fine detail brushes; 220-grit sandpaper; colored chalk; string; pencil

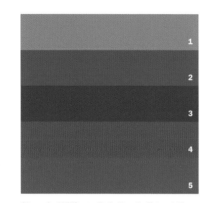

Sherwin Williams Palette: 1. Tatami Tan 2. Houseplant 3. Impulsive Purple 4. Gibraltar 5. Revel Blue

1 **Sketch the window shape.** First, consider the angle from which the window is most likely to be observed. Use that angle to determine its perspective. To draw a circle, pin a string in the center of your "window" and tie a pencil to the other end; then draw the circle with the pencil, keeping the string pulled taut. (For the scallops, I traced one half of a dinner plate.) Sketch the window design with colored chalk.

2 **Sculpt the 'slate' window frame.** Before applying the joint compound, tint it with Gibraltar so when it's sanded later, the color will bleed through to add a more realistic look to the faux slate. Using a 1 ½-inch (37mm) putty knife, carefully sculpt the individual pieces of slate framing the window with the tinted joint compound.

3 **Paint the slate.** When the mud dries, use several colors to shade and tone the slate (here, Gibraltar, Tatami Tan, Revel Blue and Impulsive Purple), with black to match the real slate in the room. Apply the colors randomly and blend using a ½-inch (12mm) square-tipped artist brush.

Let dry, then gently sand the painted slate. (This adds a sense of dimension and realistic charm to the stone.)

As a background, I suggest a subtle hint of clouds and atmosphere by mottling Revel Blue and white.

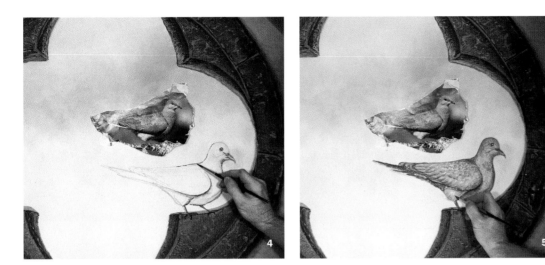

4 **Sketch the dove.** Sketch the bird with chalk, using a reference photo taped to the wall as a guide. Outline the bird using artist's fine detail brushes and the same tones used in the slate.

5 **Paint the dove.** Paint the bird using the same tones used in the slate. First, shade body with artist's brushes, gradually adding feathers and other details until you achieve the desired degree of realism. Add shadows for even greater depth and believability.

6 **Sketch and paint the ivy.** To bring a little more life to the scene, add a trailing vine of ivy. Its delicate meandering softens the surroundings.

FAUX-RUSTED VANITY

The master bath vanity is actually a standard stock 36-inch (90cm) cabinet sink base, combined with a 12-inch (30cm) base cabinet. My carpenter also built a custom wood countertop. A standard oval porcelain sink, with rubbed-bronze hardware, completes the look. I applied a galvanized, rustic metal finish to the vanity. The product does most of the work, making it a very simple finish. The deep tones add weight and richness to the overall feel of the piece. The same finish was applied to decorative molding around the base of the tub. The malleable plastic polyurethane trim was attached with construction adhesive and then finished. The rich, rusty tones are reflected in the surrounding natural slate floor and tub enclosure. To balance the high contrast of the slate and vanity with the white tub, toilet and sink, I added white porcelain and rustic iron knobs and handles as a finishing touch.

MATERIALS LIST

Magic Metallic Steel Paint and Rapid Rust patina; spray bottle; 2-inch (51mm) chip brush and/or paint roller; polyurethane

Sherwin Williams Palette: 1. French Roast

1 Prepare the surface. As with any unfinished wood furniture, seal the surface with primer. When this dries, apply a base coat of a dark, rich brown (here, French Roast).

2 Apply metallic paint. Apply the first coat of Magic Metallic over the basecoat, using a 2-inch (51mm) chip brush for the raised areas and a small roller for the flat areas.

3 Apply second coat. When the first coat dries completely, apply another coat of the metallic paint. While this second coat is still wet, apply Rapid Rust anywhere you want a rusty appearance. To make application easier, I filled a spray bottle with Rapid Rust and lightly spritzed the areas I wished to have patina. In approximately 45 minutes, the oxidation process will begin, and actual rust particles will form.

4 Seal the surface. To stop the oxidation process, the surface has to be sealed. I used a latex-based satin polyurethane (which dries quickly—enough for multiple coats in one day!—and is non-yellowing), applying three coats to the vanity for added protection and durability.

SPECIALTY PAINT

Magic Metallic Steel Paint is a specialty paint that produces fantastic results. It is very easy to apply and creates an unusual and complex-looking finish. The manufacturer also offers an excellent verdigris finish.

Texture Detail. The richly colored finish contrasts brilliantly with the cool slate tone. The iron monkey, a treasured gift from a dear friend, patiently offers a paisley hand towel. The angled mirror—though not as practical as I would like—adds an interesting perspective to the oddly angled room.

WHERE THIS STORY ENDS AND ART BEGINS

Tucked under the front eaves, just beyond the master bedroom, is my home studio. My main studio is in nearby Bellevue, Kentucky; this secluded area is for my personal artwork.

The master bedroom's drapery and faux river stone wall treatment is continued in this room. The pleated drapery is pinned into position with actual knobs (the same knobs that are used on the master bedroom cabinets). The combination of the real and the painted adds to the whimsical illusion of the setting.

My favorite accent in the studio is the antique wood frame with the bird's nest perched on top. I found the frame leaning against the back porch of the house. A mother bird decided that this was the perfect spot to build her home. And maybe she had the right idea. As with this house, I've learned that a home is what you make it!

The Personal Studio. The easel holds a self-portrait painted in oils that I completed in the early 1980's while I was pursuing my fine art's degree at Northern Kentucky University. It has significant value to me, as it was completed during a very tragic period in my life, after the unexpected death of my sister, Joyce. Painting and art has always been my saving grace over the years. When I create art, I can put my emotions onto the canvas, lightening my troubled spirit. This particular canvas, for example, is covered with grief.

"Art is one of the most personal and intimate forms, from which to express your most private inner thoughts and feelings." This is what my favorite high school art teacher, Linda Whittenburg, wrote in a treasured book that she presented to me, along with a certificate for the Outstanding Senior in Art Award.

Before. This dark, cramped space didn't look promising when it was filled with junk and painted a dingy blue, but I was able to uncover its potential and make it into a working studio space.

Details Define the Setting

Vintage furnishing. I furnished this space with a vintage wooden drafting table and a iron-and-wicker stool, along with a couple of storage pieces which safely store my many renderings and design ideas.

Arched symmetry. The rounded windows echo the Gothic arching repeated throughout the house. I painted the window casements with Tatami Tan, a color I used for most of the trim throughout the house. This subtle color goes a long way to unify the varied spaces in the house.

Color and acanthus. The carpet emphasizes the room's separate identity from the master bedroom, even as its acanthus patterns and teal and muted red colors tie it to the other rooms in the house.

Defining details. Presiding over the scene is an enormous paint brush. I've never used the brush; but when I found it at a yard sale for only a dollar, I knew I had to have it. It hangs over my drafting table and defines the space as a studio.

TERMS & TECHNIQUES

Biedermeier: Common in Neoclassical-inspired interiors, Biedermeier is a decorative style characterized by the use of rich, exotic wood grains and veneers, often accompanied by black lacquer finishes and/or gilded detailing.

blocking in: The initial stage of mural painting, where the general composition is defined and takes shape. A midtone color is commonly used for blocking in, which adds dimension and definition to the painting.

burnishing: Vigorously polishing a surface (e.g., Venetian plaster or gold leaf) to add luster.

chinoiserie

chinoiserie: Painting style that reflects Chinese motifs; commonly applied to raw silk, ceramics and furniture.

color wash: A quick, tonal application of color that adds atmospheric dimension and illusion to a surface. Color washes are usually transparent, allowing for multiple color variations as one wash covers another.

crackling: Decorative finish—achieved by using glazes and mediums—that produces a network of fine cracks on an otherwise smooth surface.

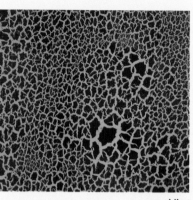
crackling

distressing: Faux-finishing technique that produces an aged appearance. Can be achieved through a variety of methods, including sanding and staining.

double load: To load a brush with two or more colors at the same time. Allows you to deposit multiple shades of color with one brushstroke.

drybrush: To lightly deposit color (as when highlighting raised detailing) by moving a barely loaded brush softly across the surface.

feather out: To gradually soften color until it blends into the surrounding area or base color. To feather out a color wash, use a 2-inch (51mm) chip brush to spread the tone until there's almost no paint left on the brush. Then, with a light touch, stroke the bristles in random directions to transition the deposited color into surrounding areas.

field tile: The most prominent tile shape, size or color in a design.

finial: A crowning ornament or detail (e.g., a decorative knob) commonly found on newel posts in older architecture.

folk art: Primitive artwork created by untrained artisans. Characteristically bold and unadorned, folk art often reflects whimsy and expressionistic use of color.

fresco: Painting on wet plaster with water-based pigments. Faux fresco refers to painting on dry plaster or compound, then painting and distressing to suggest antiquity.

frieze: Area around the perimeter of a ceiling in which a decorative border (usually raised) is applied.

frieze

glaze: Medium used to create translucent color tints and increase working (i.e., "open") time when faux finishing. Latex glaze works with water-based products; oil-glazing liquid works with oil-based products.

graining: Faux-finishing technique in which paint is manipulated with a tool to suggest wood-graining patterns.

lift color: To remove color from a particular area, such as the raised detailing in molding. Mineral spirits are used to lift oil-based products; a water-dampened rag can be used to lift water-based products.

masking

masking: Covering areas with tape to prevent paint from seeping onto them. For best results, use the appropriate tape, apply it neatly, and—when the project is complete—remove it carefully by slowly pulling it away from the surface. A hot hair dryer may be used to facilitate removal in delicate areas.

mottling: Blending one tone into another using a variety of tools, including brushes, rags and sponges. To mottle, apply random splotches of color, then use a tool dampened with water or mineral spirits to combine the tones.

mottling

mural: A specialized form of decorative painting in which a surface is painted to add illusion to the setting. Murals

140

mural

can be purely decorative and abstract, or can be painted to "fool the eye" (i.e., Trompe L'Oeil).

paint thinner: Medium, such as water or mineral spirits, used to dilute pure paint products. Specialty products, such as glazes and Floetrol, can be mixed with these mediums to further the opacity of raw pigment.

patina: Aged appearance resulting from decades of wear and tear on a surface.

pickling

pickling: Antiquing finish in which thinned white paint or glaze is applied to wood and then sanded, revealing the wood grain and leaving whitish deposits in the crevices.

pounce: To use a brush or rag to gently "punch" color onto a surface, producing a uniformly antiqued appearance.

ragrolling: A faux-finishing technique in which a rolled rag is used to remove glaze and reveal a base tone. 'Rag texturing' relies on a bunched-up rag.

ragrolling

scrub: To apply color to a surface directly from its original container, and then quickly mix it with water using rags or brushes. Commonly used in color washing.

shade: To add volume and weight to a painted object. Achieved by "dirtying" the base with dark tones to suggest shadowing.

stippling: Technique used to place paint in crevices and other hard-to-reach areas. To stipple, load a chip brush or regular house-paint brush and quickly pounce the bristles onto the surface.

strié: French term for a refined faux-finishing technique used in formal settings. In strié, a tool is moved horizontally or vertically through a glaze to reveal a pattern of delicate, silk-like threads.

strié

streaking: Creating the illusion of age or water damage on a wall. To streak, mist a painted area with water, then allow the paint to run down the walls randomly. Using more water will increase translucency.

transferring: To transfer a design to a surface. An overhead projector can be used to transfer a design directly onto a wall or onto tracing paper. To transfer using graphite paper, place the graphite paper behind the drawing and trace over it, imprinting the design on the desired surface.

transferring

transom: Small, rectangular window above a door or entryway. Common features in older, period-style homes, transoms are often composed of stained glass.

verdigris: Blue-green coating found on exposed copper and bronze objects. The result of the natural oxidation of the materials when exposed to the elements.

wainscoting: Decorative treatment below a chair rail. In period homes, wainscoting was typically composed of embossed leather or pressed tin. In modern homes, wainscoting is made from raised or recessed wood panels.

wet-on-wet

wet-on-wet: Painting technique in which colors are applied immediately on top of each other, before the previous layer has dried. When adding dimension to a leaf, for example, a midtone establishes the shape, followed by a shading tone to add dimension, and finally a highlight tone to define the light source. The colors will blend automatically, as long as paint is applied before the base tone dries.

INDEX

the best in decorative painting instruction and inspiration is from
NORTH LIGHT BOOKS!

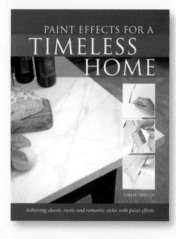

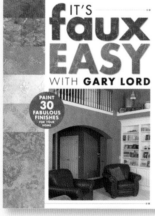

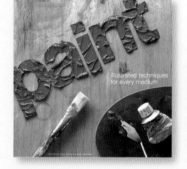

Paint Effects for a Timeless Home. With a little paint and this easy-to-follow guide, you can transform even the most modest dwellings into warm, welcoming interiors. Thirty-five step-by-step demonstrations show you how to create popular decorating styles from Tuscany, England, France, Early America and rural Mexico. Stunning photo galleries provide further decorating ideas for infusing ordinary rooms with timeless beauty, traditional artisanship and plenty of old-world appeal. ISBN 13: 978-1-58180-884-1; ISBN 10: 1-58180-884-4; paperback, 128 pages, #Z0558

Sponge Painting. Put the joy back into your painting using fast and fun technique with acrylic paints and a common household sponge! The technique is so basic, the results so remarkable and fast, that you'll soon have a home full of beautiful paintings on canvases. Choose from 20 start-to-finish painting demonstrations to create a masterpiece; each one can be finished in less than three hours. Paint a gorgeous floral still life, or a dramatic landscape scene in your favorite seasons and time of day, from early sunrise to the blue hour of early evening. Once you start painting with a sponge, you won't be able to stop! ISBN 13: 978-1-58180-962-6; ISBN 10: 1-58180-962-X; paperback 128 pages, #Z0686.

Paint. Whether you want to sharpen your painting skills, experiment with new mediums, or paint for the first time, this indispensable guide belongs by your side. Clear photos show you materials and basic techniques for each of today's most popular painting mediums. From there, move on to master essential intermediate skills, from color and composition to perspective, reference photography and many more. 15 step-by-step demonstrations let you work along with top artists from blank paper or canvas to finished painting. Paint has everything you need to begin, develop or perfect your craft. ISBN 13: 978-1-58180-970-4; ISBN 10: 1-58180-870-4, paperback, 224 pages, #Z0228

It's Faux Easy. Let master of faux finishing, Gary Lord, be your guide in creating fabulous faux finishes to accent your home's beauty. In *It's Faux Easy*, he provides easy-to-follow instructions and a no-nonsense approach to creating 30 new and unique finishes no found in other books. You'll learn how to create a variety of contemporary and traditional effects from dimensional plaster finishes with embossed or embedded stenciling to faux finishes with holographic or metallic flourishes. Full-color photography provides inspiration for designing your own painting projects. ISBN 13: 978-1-58180-554-3; ISBN 10: 1-58180-554-3, paperback, 144 pages, #33010

These books and other fine North Light titles are available at your local arts & crafts retailer, bookstore, or from online suppliers.